Silver Burdett Picture Histories
Life in Ancient Rome

Silver Burdett Picture Histories
Life in Ancient Rome

Pierre Miquel
Illustrated by Yvon Le Gall

Translated by Anthea Ridett
from La Vie privée des Hommes: Au temps des légionnaires romains
first published in France in 1978 by
Librairie Hachette, Paris

This edition published in 1980 by
The Hamlyn Publishing Group Limited
London · New York · Sydney · Toronto
Astronaut House, Feltham, Middlesex, England

Published in the United States by
Silver Burdett Company, Morristown, N.J.
1985 Printing

ISBN 0-382-06925-0

Library of Congress Catalog Card No. 80-52501

Contents

Towards the Conquest of the World

The history of Rome really began in the 8th century before Christ, when it was a tiny town in the plain of Latium. Over the next six hundred years it grew to become the centre of an Empire which ruled over the western world. By 266 BC the Romans had conquered the whole of Italy and overseas, or 'imperial', expansion began with the First Punic War in 240 BC.

VENI, VIDI, VICI?

The Strength of the Roman Army

The army consisted of 300,000 men divided into 50 legions.
Over and above this number were the auxiliaries and the cavalry:
● after Augustus's time, each Legion included 4 cavalry squadrons, totalling 120 men;
● the auxiliaries were horsemen, slingers and archers. One auxiliary cohort included 500 to 1,000 men enlisted in 6 to 10 centuries.

This Empire was not built in a day. At first Rome was ruled by kings. Then, around 509 BC, it became a Republic governed by elected magistrates. The soldiers who defended it and fought for its first conquests were not professionals but were conscripted from among the Roman people. The Legionaries who fought in the Punic Wars against Carthage in the 3rd and 2nd centuries BC were all conscripts. A hundred years later the troops that Julius Caesar led in Gaul and Britain were still mainly made up of citizens, though by that time the commander-in-chief had begun to take on paid foreign 'auxiliaries'.

PATRICIANS, PLEBEIANS AND SLAVES

The first Romans were soldiers and peasants; when they were not fighting they were struggling to cultivate their small-holdings, sowing wheat and gathering olives like all the other farming people of the ancient world. Unlike the Phoenicians and Greeks, they had no gift for sea-faring. The Roman Empire was essentially a land empire.

The lives of these peasant-soldiers were turned upside down by Rome's military conquests. For one thing, the Romans began to use their prisoners-of-war as slaves, who were sold and re-sold to wealthy owners. They were put to work on farms, in the mines, or as servants in rich households, and relieved the wealthier Romans of their heavy work and chores. But to feed, clothe and house a whole family of slaves cost money, which the small farmers did not have. They began to sell their small-holdings to the richer land-owners, and soon throughout the fertile plains of Italy simple farms were merged in great estates. At the same time Rome found that many products like wheat could be imported more cheaply from other parts of the Empire. The poorer folk flocked to Rome and other big towns, where they made up the mass of 'plebeians'. Huge numbers of them were unemployed and had to live on assistance, first from the 'patricians', the wealthy citizens, and later from the State itself.

THE HUNGER FOR CONQUEST

Julius Caesar (101–44 BC), general and dictator, brought the Republic to an end, and his successor Augustus (63 BC to 14 AD) became the first emperor. In his hands alone lay all the power of command – *imperium*, in Latin. During the first two centuries after Christ the Empire reached its maximum size.

Some of the Legionaries were well aware that there was more of Africa beyond the Sahara, but no-one had any idea that there were other continents to the west of Gaul. The Romans also knew that beyond the Rhine and Danube rivers lay huge territories overrun by nomadic German-speaking tribes of 'barbarians'. But after a disaster in AD 9 when three legions were destroyed in the Teutoburger forest in north-west Germany, Augustus gave up any idea of conquering them.

THE EMPEROR, AND OTHER GODS

At the heart of this protected world, which had inherited all the riches of the ancient civilizations that preceded it, the Emperor was endowed with limitless power. He was chief of the army and head of State, in charge of the government and law-making. He was also raised to the level of a god, and had to be worshipped as one.

The Romans already had a great many gods. They were easy-going in religious matters, and a man might adopt any religion he chose so long as its rites did not disturb public order or infringe accepted morals. The Romans' Jupiter and Neptune, for instance, were originally the Greek gods Zeus and Poseidon. Later, the Romans worshipped the Egyptian goddess Isis and the Persian god of light, Mithras; they even adopted Celtic and Germanic deities. The imposition of emperor-worship put a fatal end to this complacency. The Jewish people, and after them the Christians, were in fierce opposition to Rome on the question of religion, for they were only allowed to worship one god and rejected all others, starting with the emperor. They made it clear that they would, and

Sight-seeing in the Roman Empire

Some people travelled long distances to look at the Seven Wonders of the World, which were:

- *The mausoleum of Halicarnassus in Asia Minor*
- *The Egyptian pyramids*
- *The statue of Zeus at Olympia*
- *The Colossus of Rhodes – in fragments. It was about 30 metres high but was wrecked by an earthquake in 225 B.C.*
- *The temple of Artemis at Ephesus*
- *The Hanging Gardens of Semiramis at Babylon*
- *The great Pharos (lighthouse) of Alexandria*

regularly did, pray *for* the emperor, but *to* him they could not. There were two Jewish revolts, and it took the Romans several military campaigns to bring Judaea to heel.

THE GREAT ROMAN PEACE

Under the *Pax Romana* – the 'Roman Peace' – the Empire became increasingly unified. The provinces provided Rome with a wealth of food, metals and other goods; there was a unified system of currency and weights and measures, and trade circulated more or less freely. Large towns and seaports everywhere became important mercantile centres.

Rome itself, with a population which grew to 1,200,000 by the 2nd century, was a huge commercial centre. From Tunisia and Egypt vast quantities of wheat were imported, to be stored in the city. There were hundreds of huge warehouses full of oil, wine, salt, spices – everything needed to feed the Romans.

The growth of crafts and industries created a demand for more metals. The Romans got their tin from Britain and their gold from Spain, and later from Dacia. They worked the numerous lead and silver mines in Spain which yielded also iron, copper, mercury, cinnabar and possessed the only known vein of mica. The ore-deposits of the Aegean islands also were exploited, specially the emery of Naxos for the making of gems.

As the Empire grew, life in the lands all round the Mediterranean became increasingly similar. Townspeople throughout the Empire were familiar with Celtic pottery, fabrics from Syria and wines from Greece. Arms came from Spain and iron ploughs were forged in Gaul. All the citizens of the Empire dressed much alike, and the women wore the same kinds of jewellery. A fashion created in Rome would be followed as far afield as Alexandria in Egypt, or at the entry to the Black Sea.

The emperor's rule was as wide as the Empire, and under it justice was administered everywhere in Latin or Greek.

WHEN LATIN WAS A LIVING LANGUAGE

The Latin language was spoken everywhere – not by the peasants in places like Britain and Spain,

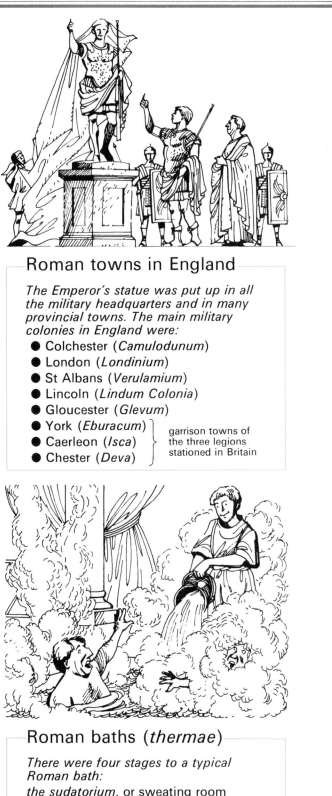

Roman towns in England

The Emperor's statue was put up in all the military headquarters and in many provincial towns. The main military colonies in England were:
- Colchester (*Camulodunum*)
- London (*Londinium*)
- St Albans (*Verulamium*)
- Lincoln (*Lindum Colonia*)
- Gloucester (*Glevum*)
- York (*Eburacum*) ⎫ garrison towns of
- Caerleon (*Isca*) ⎬ the three legions
- Chester (*Deva*) ⎭ stationed in Britain

Roman baths (*thermae*)

There were four stages to a typical Roman bath:
the sudatorium, or sweating room
the calidarium, where the sweat was washed off in warm water
the frigidarium, the refreshing cold plunge
massages and rub-downs.
In Rome the biggest *thermae* were the Baths of Caracalla (covering an area of 118,000 square metres) and the Baths of Diocletian (140,000 square metres).

of course, but their masters spoke it and sent their children to schools where the lessons were given in Latin. It was the language of the occupiers, the rulers, the rich and powerful. High-ranking men in the conquered countries had to speak it in their business and official dealings and for legal matters. It was a very effective way of uniting the different parts of the Empire. Nevertheless, among the cultivated classes, Greek maintained its primacy, and its literary pre-eminence. Every upper class Roman learned it as a child. The New Testament is a Greek book. The inscription on the Cross was written in Greek as well as in Latin and Hebrew. It was in Greek that the emperor Marcus Aurelius composed his famous meditations.

One way in which Rome maintained its power was by opening the door freely to the leading citizens of the conquered provinces. After a time Gauls and Greeks were allowed to take their seats in the Roman Senate. There were emperors who came from Spain, from North Africa and Dalmatia. The new citizens were allowed to vote, to seek office as magistrates, and to take part in the political and administrative life of the Empire.

The Pont du Gard

One of the most famous Roman aqueducts is the Pont du Gard in the south of France, 273 metres of which still stand. It was part of the system that brought water from over 20 kilometres away to supply the town of Nîmes.
It provided 20,000 cubic metres of water a day – that is, an average of 400 litres a day for each of the 50,000 inhabitants of Nîmes.

THE ROMAN GENIUS

The different parts of the Empire were not linked by language alone, important though this was. The Romans were brilliant road-builders, and 90,000 kilometres of highways ran across the Empire, always busy with travellers. They were very straight, well-defended and well-maintained; they were marked out with milestones and well supplied with inns where travellers could sleep and change horses. Many of them can be traced, even their original paving descried, in Britain today. These roads were the most important means by which Rome maintained its power.

Under the Empire an official posting service was organized, on which the speed of travel was about 80 kilometres a day. Higher speeds were attained on exceptional occasions. The Emperor Tiberius once covered 290 kilometres in a day, a speed not equalled in Europe until the nineteenth century.

However the sea, too, was important for trade. In the well-equipped seaports of the Empire, many of which were served with lighthouses, the slow Roman boats with triangular sails (now called lateen sails) or square Greek ones took on wheat and jars of olive oil. Sometimes the sea journey back from Egypt could take two and a half months; and it needed quite a lot of courage to face the Channel crossing. But in time the Romans learned to lose their fear of the sea. They even went on pleasure trips.

The Romans exported the Latin language, their building technology and their entertainments. In the big urban centres of Gaul, Africa and Spain, theatres were built and plays performed. In Britain the remains of Roman theatres have been excavated at St Albans and Canterbury. The Romans also infected the rest of their Empire with their horrifying taste for bloodthirsty spectacles. There was a flourishing trade in wild animals from Africa, so that the cruel circus 'Games' could be put on as far north as the Rhineland. Chariot racing was always popular and gladiatorial fights were held in amphitheatres at Nîmes in France, in pagan Byzantium and in Africa. The way of life in Roman cities, whether in Gaul or Africa, was almost exactly the same.

Three Hundred Thousand Legionaries

The Roman army was made up of foot-soldiers, called Legionaries; they were grouped into Legions, combat units of 6,000 men. These were divided into 10 cohorts of 600 men, and each cohort was divided into three maniples, tactical divisions of 200 Legionaries. Each maniple consisted of two centuries of one hundred men each, commanded by officers called centurions (from the Latin word *centum*, meaning 'a hundred').

Senior officers, the military tribunes who were in charge of the cohorts, and above all the Legate (*Legatus Legionis*), the overall commander of the Legion, were appointed by the emperor and took their orders direct from Rome. Special officers called Prefects were put in command of the Legions that were sent to guard the frontiers of the Empire.

In the early days of Roman history the Legions were manned by ordinary citizens who were obliged to do military service. Any Roman male between 17 and 60 could be called up, and he had to pay for his own equipment. Very soon, though, in order to build up its Legions, the State began to pay its servicemen. When Rome was the centre of an Empire, it needed a permanent force of 300,000 armed men. Augustus paid his Legionaries well, and when they retired he gave them 3,000 denarii or a plot of land to cultivate. Thus, from its peasant armies, Rome forged a highly professional force.

Under the Emperor every aspect of a Legionary's life was taken care of. He was housed, fed and clothed, and in return he had to swear loyalty to his general and submit to the harsh army discipline. Legionaries never had an idle moment. When they first joined up they were put through rigorous training, taught weapons drill and sent out on manoeuvres in the countryside, sleeping in tents and marching by day and by night. They were also taught swimming and vaulting. In addition, they had to be labourers, woodcutters, carpenters, bridge-builders and stone-masons.

The army sets up camp.

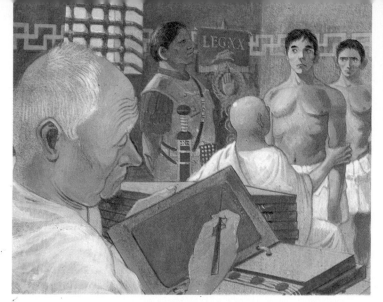

Enlisting with the 20th Legion. The surnames of the recruits were entered in a register. Then they underwent a medical examination; anyone who was ill or physically disabled was exempt from service.

Inside their barracks the Legionaries wore yellow tunics and leather helmets. This was their uniform for carrying out army fatigues – looking after the horses and mules, cleaning out the barracks, and doing their physical training (*exercitio*).

The State was responsible for feeding its soldiers. Each Legionary was allowed four bushels of corn a month – 900 grams a day – from army stores. If the stores ran out the Legionaries requisitioned corn, or harvested it themselves!

On route marches, soldiers carried their helmets round their necks and their equipment on their backs – tools, rations and bedding. Once in enemy territory, they would pillage anything else they needed. They often covered 50 kilometres a day.

Veterans, Legionaries who had completed fifteen or twenty years' service, were thanked personally by the Emperor. He rewarded them with money or plots of land; so many of them were able to spend their retirement cultivating their own small properties.

The Finest Army in the World

Legions were permanently stationed on guard along the frontiers of the Empire – which were also the frontiers of the civilized world. The Romans ruled over the Mediterranean and had pushed into Asia, and into Europe as far as the Rhine and the Danube. They built huge fortified walls, with moats, watchtowers and fortresses, to keep out the barbarians – the German tribes on the other side of the Rhine-Danube line, or the Scots north of Hadrian's Wall.

A relatively small number of Legions safeguarded the Empire. Egypt, for example, was held by only two Legions – 12,000 men. They did add to their numbers by recruiting auxiliary soldiers from foreign tribes who were brought into the cavalry; finally, auxiliaries were allowed in the Legions themselves.

When a military campaign was necessary – to put down the Numidians in North Africa, for instance, or the Germans beyond the Rhine – the Emperor would send a general with an army of two or three Legions. They marched at their fastest pace along the splendid Roman roads, to assemble at the starting point of the campaign. Once in enemy territory they would send scouts on ahead, and in the evenings they would put up a fortified camp.

In battle they always fought in the same formation, with the infantry in the centre and the cavalry on the wings. The men grouped themselves behind their standards, ready to defend them to the death. In defence, they would form into three lines and protect themselves with their shields. On the attack, they would charge in rows; first the javelin throwers flung their weapons, and then the rest went in to fight with their swords.

Victory parades called Triumphs were held in honour of victorious generals. When Caesar defeated the Gallic leader Vercingetorix, he was paraded in triumph through the richly decorated streets of Rome, from the Campus Martius (the Field of Mars) to the Capitol hill. From Augustus onwards, only Emperors had the right to take part in a Triumph.

A victorious general rides in triumph through Rome.

When a Legion captured a barbarian village, the soldiers would burn the houses and kill the able-bodied men. They carried the women and children off as slaves. Any valuable articles were pooled and divided as booty.

A Roman galley on the attack! The galley has a special gang-plank, 8 metres long, with a long spike at one end called a *corvus* – a 'crow'. This hooked on to the enemy's deck, so the Roman soldiers could rush aboard.

The Romans were not over-gentle with their victims. They made the most important prisoners march back to Rome in chains with ropes round their necks. They would then be paraded through the city in the general's Triumph.

Roman soldiers on the attack! First, the javelins were thrown; then came man-to-man fighting. Roman 'stabbing' swords were shorter than the 'slashing swords of the Celts and Germans, but they were lethal. They

were worn on the right, not the left side. The Romans were excellently protected by their helmets and their armour, and they could launch their attacks well sheltered behind their huge shields.

Engines of War

The Romans conducted their wars very scientifically, employing the services of a host of technicians, architects and engineers. They defended their towns with high, fortified walls, and once they had conquered a region they would set about building their famous Roman roads – solid, arrow-straight and paved or metalled. They built stone bridges across the rivers, too. In this way, help could be sent swiftly from one end of the Empire to the other. The Roman generals had learned from the Greeks before them a good deal about the conduct of sieges, which they brought to a fine art. In Gaul, Caesar's troops didn't begin to besiege the clumsily built enemy strongholds without a great deal of preparation; they dug ditches all around and lined them with sharp stakes, and put up their own base camp and store-rooms with a supply of rations. The town under siege was completely cut off. To get out, the Gauls would have had to besiege the Roman fortifications in turn!

The Romans were expert at capturing cities, too. They had all kinds of artillery and catapults, which could hurl stones against walls, flaming missiles against wooden gates, and arrows at the defending army. They had huge wooden rams with which they could batter down gates while they themselves were sheltered from enemy missiles. But their most effective weapon was the siege-tower, a high wooden tower on wheels, which could be pushed forward until it was right up against the enemy's ramparts. Then they would let down a kind of drawbridge, and the soldiers would charge across this straight on to the top of the walls. The sides and top of the tower were protected from flaming arrows with a covering of freshly-skinned animal hides.

The technology that went into a Roman siege prevented the enemy from getting out, but it wasn't always enough to break through strongly-built fortifications. So sieges could last a very long time. They would only come to an end when the besieged enemy were so desperate with hunger that they decided to try to get out. Then the Romans could kill or capture them.

A Roman siege-tower approaching a Gallic *oppidum* (stronghold).

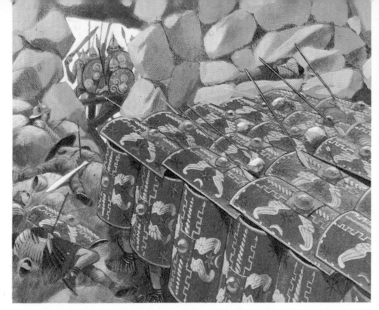

The Roman army invading a stronghold. The walls have been undermined by sappers, and the Legion is grouped in 'tortoise' formation, shoulder to shoulder, with the men in the middle holding their shields above their heads and those on the sides holding them upright.

This 'scorpion' (*scorpius*) was like a huge bow used to set fire to wooden fortifications and thatched roofs. The tips of the arrows were wrapped in rags soaked in pitch and set alight. A winch was used to draw back the bow.

Building a bridge across the Rhine, which, when finally completed, would be 400 metres long and 4 metres wide. Using sledge hammers, the Legionaries would drive fifty supporting piles into the river bed and then would lay wooden planks across them.

More Roman war machines. The catapult (*ballista*) on the left flung 59 kilogram rocks over a distance of 500 to 1,000 metres. On the right is an *onager* ('donkey'); more sturdily designed, this could hurl heavier missiles over a shorter distance.

Enormous battering rams were used to destroy the gates of enemy towns. Legionaries, protected by hide roofing, stood behind the ram, pulled it back with ropes, and then let go. The ram swung forward, battered the gates, and swung back into place.

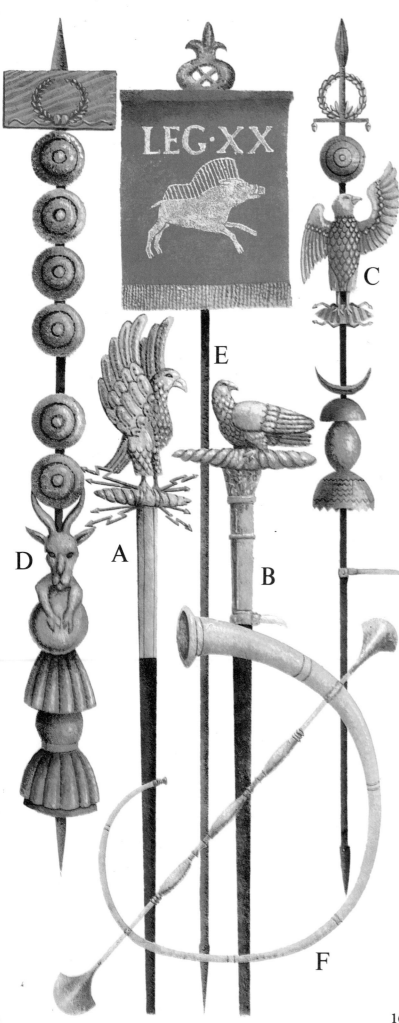

Armour and Standards

The Roman Legionary's helmet changed very little over the centuries. It was round, made of bronze, and had an iron skullcap inside it with a cloth lining. A narrow ridge across the forehead protected the nose and eyes, and widened at the back to protect the back of the neck. Two hinged cheek-pieces covered the sides of the face. The helmet was decorated with brightly coloured plumes.

From left to right: (1) Helmet worn by Tiberius's Legions (1st century AD); (2) Helmet worn by men of the 20th Legion in Nero's day; (3) Helmet from the beginning of the 2nd century AD; (4) Helmet of a Legionary of the first half of the 1st century BC.

Javelins (*pila*) were 2 to 2·10 metres long with a shaft 7 cm thick and 1·40 m long. The one on the left (5) dates from the second half of the 1st century AD; the one in the middle (6) from the 1st century BC, and the one on the right (7) from the beginning of the 2nd century AD. Each soldier carried two. The heads were of soft iron so that the weapon bent on impact and could not be thrown back.

Swords also varied in length; over the years the length was increased from 50 to 84 cm. From left to right opposite you can see a selection of swords in their sheaths (8, 9, 10, 11), all dating from the 1st century AD. The short dagger in its scabbard belongs to the same period.

Shields could be oval or oblong. The heavy oblong one (13) was carried by Trajan's Legionaries. The oval shield (14), which is lighter, dates from the reign of Tiberius. The sling (15) was used to fling lethal lead shot (16) at top speed.

Standards kept the units together in battle. The eagles (A and B) were the standards of the whole Legion, and (C) is the standard of a subsidiary unit. The designs on the maniples' standards (D) include garlands and animals. The flag of the cavalry (E) was called a *vexillum*.

(F) is a bugle belonging to Trajan's Legions. Bugle-calls were used to direct the Legion's movements.

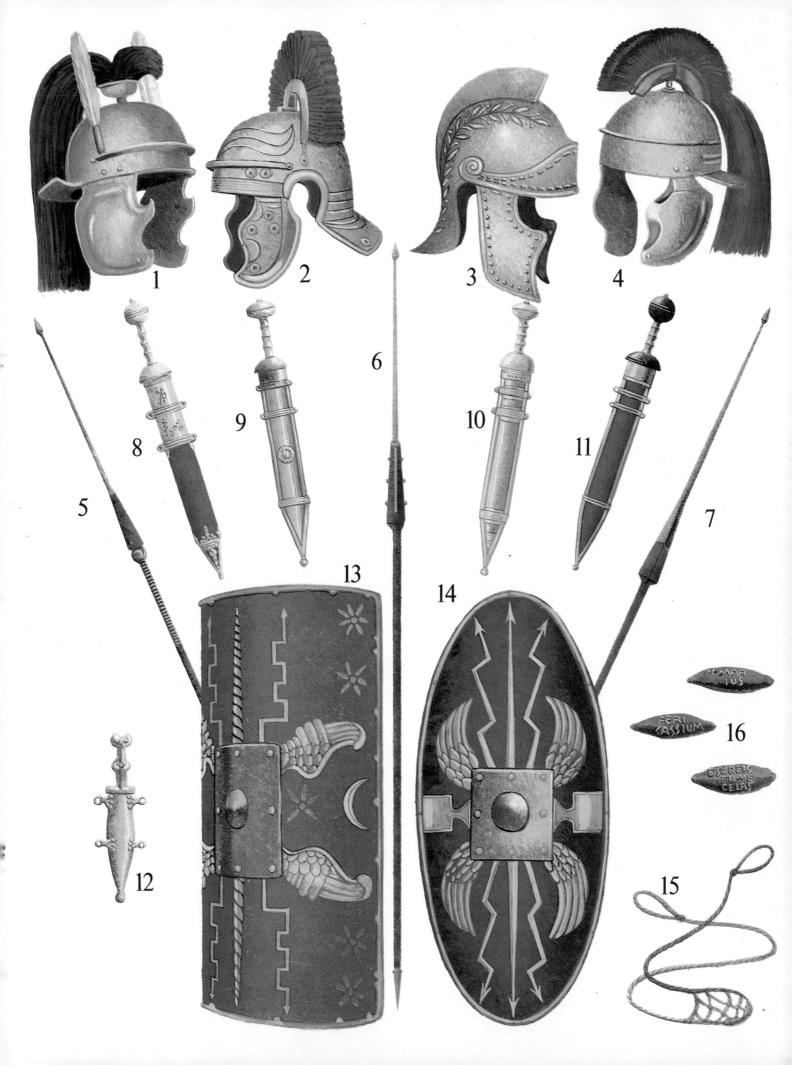

Olives, Wheat and Wine

The Romans were great city-builders. Not only in Italy, but throughout their vast empire they embellished old towns and created new ones. Roman cities were conceived on a grand scale, as the remains of so many of them proclaim. Spacious forums, lofty temples and pillars, theatres, amphitheatres, hippodromes, baths, libraries, market-places, gilded domes and statues, even stone bridges, so that the river was no longer the impassable barrier it had formerly been. The Latin for bridge-builder is *pontifex*. 'Pontifex *maximus*' became the title of Rome's high priest, and to this day it is the only pagan title still used by the Pope, the 'Supreme Pontiff'.

But, just as in the great cities of Europe and America, the growth of grandeur involved inevitable squalor. Many of Rome's citizens lived in jerry-built apartment houses, many stories high, cold in winter, stuffy in summer, with no indoor sanitation and no piped water. Romans, therefore, craved the peace and cleanliness of the country-side. Rich men owned one or more country-houses, called 'villas'. (Cicero, for instance, owned eight.) They were really the precursors of the 'plantation houses' of a later age, with their fields, their vineyards, their olive-groves and gardens, their barns and storehouses, even their slave-quarters. We know about them from existing remains.

The owners of a big estate put a manager (called a *procurator*) in charge of the work. The most profitable kinds of farming activities were rearing sheep and goats close to the towns, and horse-breeding. Agricultural knowledge was quite advanced, and fertilisers such as nitrates were already in use. The rotation of crops was understood and practised. Cultivating the fields demanded a very large work-force for a relatively low yield. An average of 47 labourers was needed to get the best out of 100 hectares of land. Only very wealthy landlords could afford to keep that many workers although some employed thousands.

The *procurator* giving out orders to the slaves on a big estate.

Rome's 'granary' included Gaul, North Africa, Sicily and Egypt. The first reaping machine was invented by a tribe living near the Moselle river. It had iron teeth which stripped the grain from the stalks; the grain then fell into a wooden container.

The Romans nearly always drank milk from sheep or goats. They planted the fields with cytisus, a shrubby plant which was useful as fodder. Cows were only found in the rainier parts of the Empire, such as Gaul and Northern Spain.

Men trod the grapes with their bare feet accompanied by the music of a flute. The most popular wines came from Greece, Cyprus, Syria and the Falernus Ager in southern Italy – Falernian wine would keep for twenty years.

The Romans did not use butter, they used olive oil for cooking and lighting. Olive oil was produced in enormous quantities – at least twenty-seven varieties of olive were known and the average profit on capital invested (2nd century BC) was about 6%.

The Roman plough was a swing-plough, largely made of wood. It comprised three sections: the shaft, which was of laurel; the stock, which was of holm oak; and the ploughshare. The ploughshare was sometimes made of oak, sometimes of bronze or iron.

Mining and Industry

Working conditions in Roman mines were appalling. They were originally worked by slaves, but later on mines were used as places of punishment for those who broke the law, particularly Christians who refused to worship the emperor as a god. In the dank underground galleries or the blazing heat of open quarries, men used to fall like flies and die very quickly.

The Romans travelled a long way to obtain metals. Long before the Romans, foreign expeditions had visited Britain looking for tin, and it was probably to get control of her tin-mines that Caesar first sent his Legionaries there. Sometimes the Romans went to war to get hold of mineral deposits. The Emperor Trajan fought the Dacians (now Romanians) for possession of their gold-mines. And Spain was one of the first countries to be conquered by Rome, as already mentioned, because of its rich mineral resources, which included lead, copper, tin, iron and mercury.

Most mines were underground. The shafts were not as deep as those of today, but they were very badly lit and ventilated. The galleries were hardly ever shored up with props, and they were very low – scarcely a metre high. The miners had to do their work crouching or lying down.

Their tools were very basic: hammers for breaking rocks, picks, shovels and wedges. They had to carry the ore out on their backs in baskets. Sometimes they washed it out with jets of water, as in gold mines, using water wheels fitted with scoops for drainage. The baskets of ore were lifted to the surface by hoists and pulleys.

The work was just as hard in the open-air quarries. The rocks were cut out in tiers, and blocks of stone would be roughly hewn on the spot, before being taken away. Then they were loaded on to boats or wagons, and transported to the building sites where they were needed. Transporting the stones was a longer more difficult and more costly job than actually quarrying them.

An open-air stone quarry.

Salt-pans at places like Ostia were a big source of revenue. They were owned by the State, but were worked by private companies. Salt was used much more than it is today, particularly for preserving meat and fish.

A lead mine in Spain. The gallery is lit by oil lamps and, unusually, is shored up by beams. Many of the slaves who worked in mines like this died of diseases caused by breathing the lead-poisoned air.

The Romans used two sorts of tiles, flat ones alternating with semi-circular ones. They can still be seen on roofs today, especially round the Mediterranean. The tiles were shaped in moulds, baked in a kiln, and dried in the open air.

Raw wool was boiled in water and pig's fat, then it was beaten, cleaned by hand and carded with a curve-toothed comb. It was woven on hand-looms in the Imperial factories. For coloured cloth, the wool was dyed before being woven.

In the quarries marble or limestone for building temples and monuments was divided into huge blocks by pushing wooden wedges into holes, and then spraying these with water. The water made the wood swell so that the pressure split the stones.

Aqueducts, Fortresses and Temples

The Romans were the foremost builders of the western world. Some of their huge, amazingly durable buildings are still standing today. For they were not just stone-masons: they were also architects and engineers.

The Romans had their own sort of cement with which they were able to make a kind of concrete – very different from the concrete used today, but nonetheless extremely tough. To build a wall, they would first of all outline the foundations with wooden planks. Between these they poured a layer of cement on which they spread a mixture of broken stones and chippings. The wall was built up with these alternate layers of concrete and chippings. After that it was dressed with a layer of narrow bricks and faced with reddish cement, which might be decorated with painted frescoes or carved reliefs, or given a rich marble facing. Rare coloured marbles were imported even from North Africa. Stucco was extensively used, to simulate marble.

The Romans often used brick for their big buildings, but they also employed materials which they found locally – the tufa stone of the Roman hills, travertine stone from the Tibur region, (hard, yellowish stone in which the Colosseum was built), limestone in Africa, and so on. They had all kinds of lifting equipment to get the blocks of stone into position and build walls of dressed stones held together with cement. Houses were generally built of a combination of wood, concrete and bricks. Pieces of Roman brick walls can be seen in parts of England today. Stone was reserved for large public buildings, like the eleven aqueducts which supplied Rome with drinking water. The Romans built aqueducts close to all the big towns like the Pont du Gard in France.

It is estimated that aqueducts furnished Rome with twelve hundred million litres of water a day. That would give about 900 litres a head. The equivalent figure for London is less than one third of the Roman ration.

An aqueduct being built.
(Above: Cross section of the water being carried through a tunnel showing the pipes and water-raising siphons.)

Workmen tiling the roof of an apartment block. Tiling methods were the same then as now. Flat tiles were placed in the gaps and round ones covered the beams. Today these tiles are often combined in a single tile, called a pantile.

Enormous cranes were used to place the blocks of stone that went into the construction of temples. The shaft was controlled by ropes, and the stones were lifted by a system of hoists and pulleys which could manoeuvre very heavy loads.

The Romans were great builders and exploited all the available stone quarries. They needed stone to build their roads, aqueducts and public buildings. Sometimes, when they were building temples, as noted above, they had marble brought from very far away.

Legionaries did a lot of building and the garrisons were always at work strengthening town fortifications. Here the men are putting up a stone wall. The blocks of stone are held together with iron cramps sealed with lead.

The Romans knew how to build stone arches, and huge domes like that of the Pantheon. The ceiling was ornamented with huge wooden panels which were covered with a layer of plaster or stucco and then decorated with sculpture or paintings.

Workshops of all kinds

The iron-workers of Britain and Gaul had nothing to learn from the Romans. For generations the Celtic tribes who lived in these countries had been using charcoal to smelt iron ore in their simple furnaces, using bellows to keep them aglow. The Celts had been mining and forging iron for four or five centuries before Caesar and his Legions invaded Gaul and Britain.

Iron was used for barrel hoops, and to make swords; although iron horseshoes had not yet been invented, the Celts made two-wheeled ploughs with iron wheels and shares. The ancient Roman ploughs inherited from the Greeks had wooden blades which were not strong enough to work the corn-rich but heavy soil of northern Gaul and Britain. The Romans later introduced iron or bronze ploughshares for working heavy soils.

The earth itself provided craftsmen with raw material in the form of clay. Italian and Gallic potters were no less skilled than the iron-workers. Pottery *amphorae* (jars) were used to transport oil, wine and grain, and to store household foods. The potters made oil-lamps of terra cotta (baked earth) and finely decorated vases and statuettes. All these everyday Roman articles, generally made in good quality clay from Gaul, could be found on any street stall in the towns and cities of the empire.

The big towns were bustling with all kinds of trades and crafts. Small shops opened out into the streets, and there were wine and oil merchants, butchers and bakers, stores selling silks and fabrics, dyers and embroiderers, ivory carvers and jewellers, silversmiths and goldsmiths . . .

And all these goods had to be carried on people's backs through the narrow streets of Rome, which were jam-packed with porters, pedlars and street salesmen. Wagon-drivers could not get their heavy vehicles past, and muleteers had problems weaving their way through the crowd with their trains of pack-animals. Slaves hurried through the congested streets and the rich picked their way through the swarming crowds, carried by litter.

A Celtic blacksmith. His bellows are made of goatskin.

A pottery in Gaul. The unrefined clay was moistened and kneaded by hand (right), thrown on the wheel (left), and the pots fired in a kiln. Vases were usually decorated before they were fired, although they were sometimes painted afterwards.

A baker's stall, with the oven behind it. This baker is selling top quality bread – loaves made from pure wheat-flour, the crust coated with egg-white and sprinkled with aniseed or cumin. Poor people usually ate bread made of barley or millet.

The Romans nearly always wore garments made of woollen cloth which they bought at the draper's. The cloth varied in fineness and quality, and was sometimes dyed in bright colours. Ladies preferred to wear linen.

The wine-merchants district lay on the banks of the Tiber near the Aventine Hill, where a huge permanent store of wine, imported from Mediterranean countries, was kept. Many wine merchants ran *tabernae* (inns), but women were forbidden to drink in them.

A Legionary getting a cobbler to put studs in the soles of his leather shoes, to prevent them from wearing out so fast on stony ground and paved roads. Shoemakers also made boots for riding, and sandals.

A sculptor's workshop.

The Artists of Rome

The Romans were extremely fond of bas-reliefs, pictures carved in stone or, supremely well, in stucco. It was a technique they had learned from the Greeks, and their artists were very good at it. A great deal of what we know about the Romans comes from these stone pictures of all aspects of their life.

The emperors and high officials ordered carvings of military victories to be put up on columns or triumphal arches. Two very famous ones still standing are the Arch of Titus, which is decorated with scenes celebrating the future Emperor Titus' victory over the Jews, and Trajan's Column, which tells the story of Trajan's campaigns in Dacia. The sculptors used all their skills to make these scenes look life-like; they show warships, charging cavalry, Legionaries standing on the ladders they have put up against the ramparts of the town under attack, and prisoners of war being brought back in chains.

The sculptors had private customers, too, for whom they carved scenes from ordinary life. A shoemaker might ask to be portrayed with all his tools or a husband would order a tomb showing him with his wife. Sculptures like these were sent all over the Empire in their tens of thousands.

Painters were less in demand than sculptors. But there was one fashion which became very popular: people had the walls of their rooms decorated with huge frescoes, wall-paintings showing scenes from mythology, geometrical designs, and still lifes.

Roman artists had many other skills, too. They were past masters in the art of carving cameos, small stones engraved with all kinds of subjects (portraits, scenes from legends, battles, etc.). And the rich, who were very fond of entertaining, had magnificent dinner services made, often in silver, like the Milden-hall Treasure dug up in Suffolk and now in the British Museum, which must have been exported to a rich family living in Britain in the 4th century. The Romans also knew how to make beautiful glassware and fine ceramics. They inherited this taste for beauty in everyday objects from the Greeks.

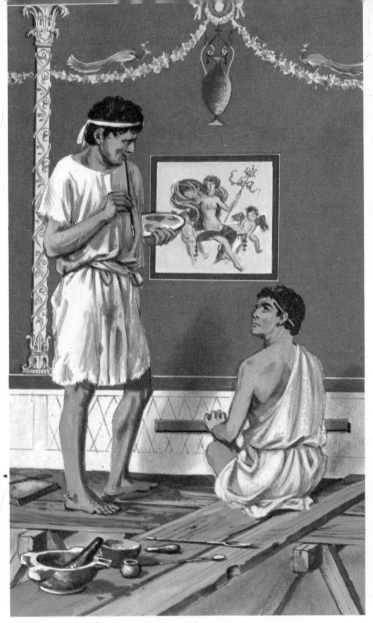

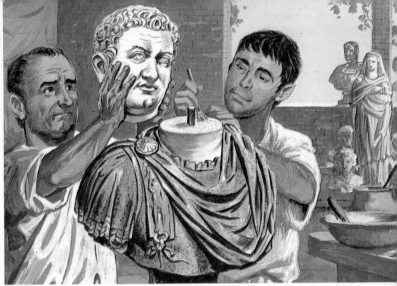

All the Roman emperors had sculptures made of themselves. They also used their coinage to let their subjects know what they looked like. Before the invention of printing, the circulation of coins was the fastest and most effective way of relaying information.

The painter's assistant would grind pigments in a mortar to make paints. There were four basic colours: white, yellow, red and black, and the colours had to be mixed slowly and carefully to produce the shade the artist wanted.

These few examples can give you only a faint idea of the amazingly rich output achieved in the field of minor arts. These beautiful objects made life very agreeable for wealthy Romans, and they are the mark of a civilization where artistic talent was combined with imagination and technical skill.

The Romans excelled at mosaics, a skill they learned from the Greeks. First the artist worked out his design on the floor, then placed the thousands of little cubes of coloured marble, which make up the mosaic, stuck down by a special cement.

1 A cameo

2 A delicate glass jug

3 A ring made by a Roman jeweller

4 A gold bracelet

5 A chased silver chalice

6 A bronze oil lamp

Living in Rome

There were 1,200,000 people to be housed in ancient Rome, so the builders had plenty of problems. Most Roman towns were carefully planned and laid out in a grid-pattern, but Rome grew out of the small villages on its seven hills which spread to meet in the centre, and it was a jumble of winding streets. As the city grew the plebeians could no longer live inside the city walls, and they were crowded into squalid houses in the working-class districts.

The very rich owned palaces or mansions with gardens, swimming pools, interior court-yards and arcades. But to house the poor, *insulae* were built – apartment blocks several storeys high, not unlike our modern blocks of flats. They were built in a square shape round a central courtyard. Augustus decreed that they should not be more than 20 metres high. But the population of Rome went on growing, and some people built veritable skyscrapers, like the Insula of Felicula, which was one of the sights of the city.

The 45,000 apartment houses had no modern conveniences. The only heating consisted of charcoal stoves, and water had to be carried from the ground floor or from street fountains. Some of the houses were built on the sides of the hills, while others were clustered closely to-gether in the unhealthy parts of the city near the Tiber.

In these over-crowded buildings a fire could be a real disaster. The fire-fighters could not get through the narrow, cluttered streets quickly, and they never had enough water to put out a big blaze. The Great Fire of 64 AD was a major catastrophe, killing thousands of people, and during the reign of Antoninus Pius, in the 2nd century AD, 340 houses were destroyed in a single day.

The streets and alleys of Rome ran to a total of 85 kilometres. Only the main roads which crossed the city – the Via Sacra (Sacred Way), Via Ostiensis (Ostian Way) and the Via Latina (Latin Way) – were paved and kept clean and in good repair. The narrow alleys were badly lit, muddy and dirty. The few streets that had pavements were cluttered with stalls and make-shift shops.

A busy Roman street.

Roman apartment blocks had no running water. Water from aqueducts could only flow to ground-floor level. The tenants on the upper storeys were supplied by water carriers, or had to fetch and carry for themselves.

The Romans really dreaded fire. Anyone who deliberately set fire to a building was burnt at the stake, while the punishment for causing a fire by accident was a public flogging. Rome had its own fire-brigade with fire-fighting equipment.

There were plenty of inns (tabernae) in Rome, where men could drink wine (they always drank it watered down) and play dice. They had plenty of leisure, for the working day finished at noon, and many Romans were permanently unemployed.

A Roman market. You would be able to recognize quite a lot of the produce on the stalls – but there were no tomatoes or potatoes. People could buy green vegetables, pulses, fruit from the neighbouring country-side, meat, salted fish and wild game.

Workmen are using pulleys to put up a statue called the Colossus of the Sun. It was a huge bronze sculpture of the sun-god, with the face of the Emperor Nero. Later the great amphitheatre called the Colosseum was built nearby.

Home and Family Life

Roman girls were usually married very young – between twelve and fifteen – and weddings were elaborate affairs. The bride wore a saffron wedding gown and a flame-red veil over her hair, with a garland over it. After the religious ceremony and the wedding feast, a procession led her to her new home; as they went, nuts were thrown to children as a symbol of fertility. Three of the groom's friends brought the bride in; the best man brandished a torch of twisted hawthorn twigs while the other two lifted her over the threshold. Inside, the walls were draped with white and the pillars decorated with laurel and ivy leaves, symbolizing health and strength. Three friends of the bride followed her in, one carrying a distaff and one a spindle. The husband came in last, with the rest of the wedding party, and offered the bride fire and water. Then the third maid of honour led her to her bedchamber.

The man was absolute master of the household. In the early days of the Republic a father had total power over his children's lives. He could refuse to recognize them and could sell them into slavery, or even kill them. Gradually, laws were introduced to protect children, and women, too, against abuses by these all-powerful husbands and fathers. As time went on, some patrician women began to make violent demands for equality, dressing up as men and taking part in chariot races though they were forbidden to appear in the amphitheatres. Some women were well-educated and took a keen interest in law, politics and literature. If the husband did not approve it was fairly easy for a woman to get a divorce and go home to her parents. If a husband rejected his wife she had the right to ask for the return of her dowry.

While children were small they were cared for by their mother or a nurse, but in wealthy families they were soon placed in the hands of a tutor (*paedogogus*), who would be an educated slave or freedman. The children of the poor grew up in the streets as best they could.

A bride being carried over the threshold of her new home.

Every family had its shrine dedicated to the *Lars familiaris*, the guardian of the home. The serpent above the altar was a symbol of strength and fertility. The father would lead the family in prayers and daily offerings.

There were no hospitals in Rome, and women had their babies at home, seated in chairs, and assisted by often ill-trained midwives. In difficult cases a doctor would probably be called, or even a surgeon, who might use his forceps.

The *tonsor* is shaving a young man's first growth of beard and carefully gathering up the hairs, watched by the whole family. This ceremony took place when the young man had grown enough beard, so there was no fixed age for it.

The heart of the Roman household was the *atrium*, and guests were received there. The *atrium* was a large chamber open in the centre to the sky. Rainwater fell through the opening, (*compluvium*), and was collected in a tank beneath (*impluvium*).

This young man has died, and his body laid out in a life-like pose. Professional mourners were hired to weep and wail, and cypress branches were placed outside to inform passers-by that there had been a death in the house.

Small Meals and Big Banquets

Generally speaking, town-dwellers did not eat very well. The diet of ordinary Romans consisted mainly of starchy foods, including a kind of wheat porridge, and little in the way of green vegetables, fresh meat or fats. It was not a balanced diet and many children suffered from malnutrition. Most people made do with a glass of water and a piece of bread rubbed with garlic for breakfast, and at midday they ate a frugal, uncooked meal. They had a bigger, cooked meal in the evening.

The wealthy and the greedy paid particular attention to the *cena*, the big evening meal when the family got together, often with friends. In large Roman mansions the kitchens were enormous, thronged with an army of slaves who were always busy preparing huge feasts.

In summer these great banquets usually came to an end before sunset, but there were times when they went on all night. The guests lay on couches which were placed around the table. They used spoons to serve themselves and knives to cut their meat, and they also made heavy use of toothpicks. But they had no forks, and ate with their fingers.

Banquets would include at least seven courses. The first course (*gustatio*) was followed by three *entrées*, two joints of meat, and dessert (*secundae mensae*). The *entrées* were substantial – fowl, kidneys, sows' udders (a dish the Romans relished), hares, or fish. The meat dishes included young boars, roasted, and boiled calves.

At the beginning of the meal the guests drank honeyed wine and tasted all the dishes, accompanied with little hot rolls. The cork or clay stoppers would be removed from the wine-jars and the wine poured out into big bowls and mixed with water. The guests would be served from these bowls by the slaves who were in constant attendance.

This kind of banquet was exceptional, however. Most evening meals were much more modest. They always followed the same plan: olives, tunny or anchovies to start with; a single main dish, such as roast kid, and then a dessert.

The kitchen of a wealthy Roman household.

Plebeians mainly ate beans, chickpeas and cabbage soup cooked with lard. There was one main dish for the whole family. Their bread was very coarse, and their wine, which was watered down, had to be filtered before they drank it.

The *prandium* or mid-day meal was frugal, even for the rich. Cheese, fruit and bread dipped in wine staved off hunger until the evening meal, the *cena*. Sometimes hot dishes were eaten, but these were usually leftovers.

The Romans did not sit down to the *cena* in the evening – they lay down. Guests helped themselves with their fingers. They were provided with napkins, but according to some writers they sometimes used their slaves' long hair to wipe their hands.

Bakers ground their own flour in heavy stone mills worked by slaves. They bought the grain from stores owned by the State, and supplied these stores with the bread which was distributed free to the plebeians.

Education – Reading, Writing and Public Speaking

Elementary schools for ordinary Roman children were dismal places. They were often held in single rooms or small booths, shut off from the street by nothing but a curtain, disturbed by the noise of traffic and freezing cold in winter. The schoolmaster, the *magister*, was often not well-educated himself; he had too many pupils and was poorly paid. These schools were attended by both boys and girls, including slave children, between the ages of seven and fifteen. They were taught to read, write and count, using an abacus or counting frame. The schoolmaster did not spare the rod, and children were often savagely beaten for misdemeanours.

The Romans were not too concerned about educating their poor or the people of their conquered nations, so long as the children of high-ranking families got a good education. These children would first be taught to read at home by a *paedogogus*, an educated slave or freedman, until their early teens when they went on to secondary education. They were taught, in both Latin and Greek in these schools, set up in Rome and the big provincial towns, by the *grammaticus* – the grammarian. Only a privileged few, and only boys, received this kind of education. Their professors came from places like Athens, Pergamum and Rhodes, where the Greeks had established a tradition of education; some of them came from Alexandria in Egypt. The grammarian taught literature (both Greek and Latin), history, geography, music and mythology – and very little in the way of mathematics. For higher education boys were sent on to the *rhetor*, the rhetorician, where their studies consisted almost entirely of learning to speak in public and to write good letters. This education was designed for the sons of senators.

Although the Romans were excellent mining and building engineers, there was no formal education in technical or scientific subjects. This kind of knowledge was passed down from father to son, and by masters to apprentices.

An elementary school in Rome.

Any boy who wanted to become an *aedile* (a public official) or a senator had to learn the art of public speaking. He learnt the speeches of the great Roman orators by heart and could recite them as well as being fluent in both Latin and Greek.

Text-books were manuscripts carefully transcribed onto rolls of papyrus by copyists, who were usually slaves. The works of Greek scholars, philosophers and doctors were copied for Roman schoolchildren as well as Latin authors.

Roman children played at knucklebones (on the right), as well as a kind of hockey. They enjoyed playing with hoops, dolls and other toys, and

they knew all kinds of ball-games, using apples, nuts, or balls made of leather stuffed with bran.

Roman children copied their lessons using a stylus on a wooden tablet covered in wax. Some tutors made learning fun, using slaves as sandwich

men and letters made of pastry to help their pupil master the 24 letters of the Roman alphabet.

Baths, Hygiene and Medicine

Public baths, called thermae, were very popular with the Romans. They were run on much the same principle as saunas today – starting with a hot steam bath, and finishing with a cold plunge. *Thermae* were built by the public authorities and entrance to them was free. It was forbidden for men and women to bathe together; they had to go at separate times of day.

In the city of Rome alone there were several hundred *thermae*, some of them very large. The baths of Diocletian (whose ruins can be seen today) covered an area of thirteen hectares. Around the baths themselves were porticoes, exercise grounds and rooms where people could play ball-games, including a kind of tennis, using the palm of the hand as a racquet. There were gymnasia, too, and even libraries.

Romans, then, were very conscious of personal hygiene and cleanliness. There was a government department in charge of the city water supply and the maintenance of aqueducts, and officials supervised the baths and drainage.

The Romans also paid a lot of attention to their health. As well as bathing and exercising they wasted a lot of money on the many charlatans who promised them 'miracle' cures and pretended to be specialists in particular diseases. Proper medical knowledge was very limited. Galen, the celebrated Greek physician, once remarked: 'The only difference between Roman doctors and Roman brigands is that the doctors kill people off in the towns and the brigands in the country.' However, there were conscientious doctors, too, particularly the followers of Galen. Some surgeons were skilled at performing quite delicate operations, including setting fractures, amputating limbs, fitting artificial legs, and even trepanning – an operation which involves making a hole in the patient's skull. But specialists like these were very rare, and their services expensive.

The poor country folk hardly ever went to see town doctors. They used healers and herbalists, and their own folk-remedies.

Inside a Roman bath: the frigidarium or cold bath.

Plan of the Baths of Caracalla in Rome.

1. Calidarium
2. Tepidarium
3. Frigidarium
4. Exercise ground
5. Gymnasia
6. Libraries

Wealthy ladies had slaves to dress their hair, using curling tongs and pins to keep the curls in place. They often wore wigs (made from the hair of slaves or imported from Germany) and used makeup to enhance their complexion.

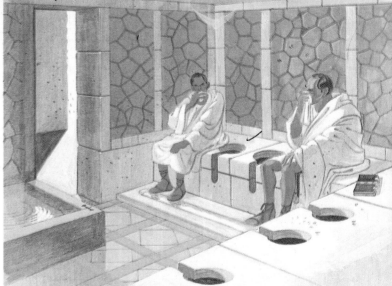

Towns were provided with *forica*, public lavatories. At Dougga in Tunisia one was found which could seat 26 people. They would sit and chat to each other without embarrassment. Running water carried the waste to the main drains.

Most Roman medicines were made from herbs. Over 500 known plants were used, the commonest being hellebore, verbena, foxglove and lime-flower. Some quack medicines were made of extraordinary ingredients – snake's venom, gladiator's blood or animal dung.

Some of the instruments used by Roman doctors and surgeons. 1. Speculum. 2. Pincers. 3. Enema. 4. Cupping glass. 5, 5B. Scalpels. 6. Hook for drawing apart the edges of a wound. 7. Instrument for piercing holes. 8. Forceps. 9. Clip. 10. Forceps. 11. Saw-blade. 12. Lever for holding up broken bones.

Children often suffered from malnutrition and were often the innocent victims of terrible epidemic diseases like typhus. Some doctors, often freedmen (former slaves), travelled from town to town, offering their medical services at fairs and markets.

It was quite usual for barbers to act as doctors and surgeons. This man is being treated for a head-wound; the barber has first shaved the man's head and is now using a spatula and spoon to dress the wound with a poultice, made to his own recipe.

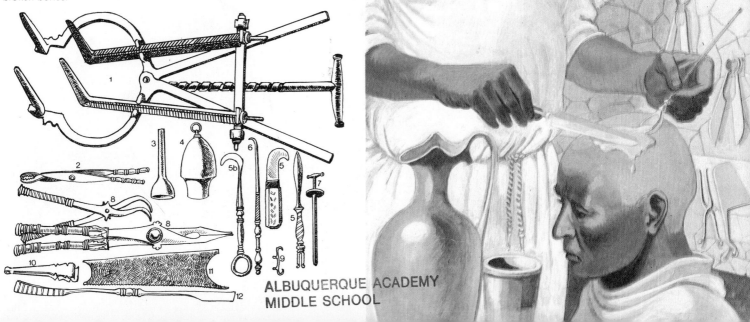

Entertainment for all

While the plebeians flocked to the amphitheatres and hippodromes, far fewer people went to the theatre, and they tended to be more choosy. Of course the theatres of Rome could only seat 60,000 compared with the 250,000 places available to the fans of chariot racing in the Circus Maximus alone. All the same, Roman theatres were very big compared with ours today.

All the best Roman comedies and tragedies – the classics by writers like Plautus and Terence modelled on the Greek playwrights – were written before the end of the Republic. After that, the shows became more and more grandiose, with complicated scenery, but the plays themselves were mimes, pantomimes and knockabout farces. The performers had to be able to sing, mime, or do acrobatic tricks, accompanied by flutes and citherns. The theatre became more and more of a mass spectacle.

Even without going to the theatre there were plenty of distractions in the streets of Rome – and probably of Constantinople and London, too. In the markets and under the porticoes idle Romans were entertained by travelling performers – musicians, clowns, acrobats and jugglers, animal-tamers – all competing with beggars for coins from the curious crowds. And people would amuse themselves by playing knucklebones, dice, or other games of chance, for money. And in the evenings they could meet and drink at the *tabernae*, the inns, which were always popular.

More select amusements – dancing, music, poetry recitals and play readings – took place in private, in the mansions of the wealthy. Patricians kept their own performers, who often lived in their houses. Virtuosi of the harp or the cithern were very much in demand; they lived like princes and could command fabulous fees – the Emperor Vespasian paid 200,000 sesterces for one cithern concert. But such privileged artists were very rare. Great art was for those who could afford to pay professionals; it didn't reach the man in the street.

A comedy being performed on the stage of a big Roman theatre

Choosing a mask. In the Roman theatre, there were standard masks for all the characters and an actor might play a young girl, an old man and a slave, in the same play. Masks were made of rags covered in plaster and painted colourfully.

With all the gambling that went on, precautions were taken against cheating. Dice-shakers had circular ridges inside so that the dice were properly shaken before being played. The Legionaries, particularly, played dice a great deal.

Theatre seats were reserved, or rented out. Sometimes people would gatecrash from outside, and the manager would have to take the law into his own hands; he would get his slaves to turn the trouble-makers out, using force if necessary.

City streets were enlivened by travelling musicians playing brass cymbals, double flutes, pan-pipes and tambourines. They were not allowed to play trumpets or horns because they were regarded as ceremonial instruments.

Wealthy Romans held concerts in their palaces. The cithern (in the foreground) has a tortoise-shell sounding board. The hydraulic organ (centre) was worked by water. under pressure, forcing air through the pipes.

Gladiatorial Contests

Gladiators were armed men who fought each other to the death for the amusement of the public. The Romans loved these bloodthirsty 'games' and their rulers, starting with Caesar and followed by Augustus and the emperors after him, made themselves popular by turning these contests into national institutions. All over the Empire, amphitheatres sprang up like the Colosseum in Rome, which could hold 50,000 spectators. A law made it obligatory for town authorities to organize games – *munera* – in their arenas.

In Rome, the emperor himself was responsible for organizing the games, assisted by his officials. In provincial cities, however, the magistrates had to hire the services of specialist contractors. They would buy men at slave auctions, or recruit them from the poor. Some were even volunteers, attracted by the prospect of reward. These men were then put through a rigorous training in special schools. In Rome, the emperor's gladiators were chosen from prisoners of war or criminals who had been condemned to death.

The spectacle began with fights between wild animals, brought from all over the Empire. A rhinoceros might be pitted against an elephant, or a bear let loose among buffalo. And the sand in the arena flowed red with blood. But what the public really appreciated was the gladiatorial contests. On the evening before, the contestants were treated to a public banquet, and on the day itself they paraded round the arena. As they passed the emperor's box they called out, '*Ave Caesar morituri te salutant.*' 'Hail, Emperor! We who are about to die salute thee!' During big festivals thousands of gladiators took part. They were paired off by drawing lots. The public laid bets and followed the duels with bloodthirsty excitement. When a gladiator fell the victor looked to the emperor for a decision. If the emperor raised his thumb the fallen man was allowed to live; if he pointed his thumb downwards, he would die.

The emperor raises his thumb and a fallen gladiator is reprieved.

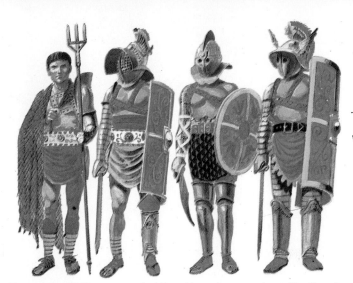

The *retiarius* (left) was armed with a trident, dagger and net. The Samnite, heavily armed, carried a shield and short sword. The Thracian, carried a round buckler and a dagger; lastly the *myrmillo*, with an oblong shield fought with the *retiarius*.

The Romans were thrilled by fights between wild animals. Here a bull is trying to gore an elephant. The bull was roped to a heavy ring so that he could not avoid the charging elephant, who was ridden by a trainer.

The *bestiarius* was a gladiator who specialized in fighting animals. During the Empire thousands of men and animals died for the amusement of the Roman public who really enjoyed the sight of blood.

A winning gladiator would have gifts lavished on him, and women would try to touch him – like pop-stars today. It was forbidden for the public to set foot in the arena, and they would be quickly chased out by an arena official.

Prisoners who had been condemned to death were tied naked to stakes and left to famished lions, some even being pushed on trollies towards the ravenous beasts. Many Christians died like this during the persecutions which followed their refusal to worship the emperor.

Bread and Circuses!

The vast numbers of poor and unemployed people in Rome were a danger to the State. To prevent them from becoming too restless, their rulers tried to keep them happy by providing them with *'panem et circenses'* – 'bread and circuses'. Every month they were handed out a free ration of flour. And more and more entertainments were provided for them in amphitheatres and circuses – for they always had time to go to a show. At one time there were nearly 200 public holidays a year, in honour of religious festivals, the emperor's birthday and military victories – Caesar's invasion of Britain was celebrated with twenty days' public holiday!

Many of these celebrations were very cruel. At the festival of the 'October Horse' for instance, on 15th October, a horse-race was held in the Forum. The winning horse was sacrificed to the god Mars and its head displayed by the Via Sacra.

Circuses were nothing like the Circuses we know today. They were U-shaped arenas in which chariot-races were held. The biggest was the Circus Maximus; with a track 1,200 metres round. The chariots had to cover seven laps in a race – 8,400 metres in all.

A magistrate gave the starting signal by dropping a white handkerchief, and the *quadrigae* – two-wheeled, four-horse chariots – were off in a cloud of dust. The *aurigae*, the charioteers, stood upright, protected by helmets and leather thongs round their thighs and legs. There were turning posts at each end of the track; it was only too easy to crash into these, and accidents could be fatal.

Winning charioteers became idols and earned a lot of money. One of them, Aurelius Mollicius, had won over a hundred races at the age of twenty. A charioteer who survived long enough to retire would have one to three thousand wins to his credit. Very few, though, lived long enough to enjoy their winnings. Chariot racing was more dangerous than motor-racing today.

At the end of the day's races (usually ten or twelve in all) the emperor might provide a feast for the crowds, and hand out small gifts to them.

A chariot race in the Circus of Caligula in Rome.

Chariots went so fast that the iron rims of the wheels got hot enough to set fire to the wood. Circus employees would throw water to cool them down. The *auriga* wore a tunic in his team's colours, and rode with the reins wrapped round his body.

Betting outside the entrance to the Colosseum, where the gladiatorial contests were held. The Romans loved gambling, and laid bets on gladiators as well as charioteers. At the races they bet on four rival teams – green, white, blue and red.

A *naumachia* was a mock naval battle, a very lavish and bloodthirsty form of entertainment which was put on on special occasions. They were held in amphitheatres flooded with water. The first *naumachia* in Rome was organized by Caesar, who had a pool dug in the Campus Martius and filled with water from the Tiber. The opposing ships contained 2,000 combatants, all prisoners-of-war or condemned criminals, who had to fight as if it was a real battle.

Sometimes arenas were filled with real rocks and greenery for the staging of mock hunts (*venationes*). The trees would be dripping with gold and perfumed fountains played. The animals were let out, and the huntsmen attacked. They were protected with armour, and if things got too dangerous they could slip into one of the partitioned turnstiles or dive inside a basket fitted with spikes. The tiers of the Colosseum would be full of people eager to watch lions, panthers, elephants and even crocodiles. On the day the Colosseum was officially opened, 5000 animals were killed.

'In the Name of the Senate and the Roman People'

The men who sat in the Senate were the highest ranking Roman citizens. During the Republic the senators played an important role in the government. Their task, like that of members of parliament today, was to discuss government policy, and finances, recommend war or peace, and approve or reject new laws. Of course, they didn't always agree among themselves. Senators who disagreed with someone would cover their heads with the sleeves of their togas.

During the Empire the Senate began to lose its power. From Augustus onwards, the Emperor was the real master. He might make a show of listening to what the senators had to say, and official pronouncements always included the words 'In the name of the Senate and the Roman people'. But the Emperor always got his own way. The Senate had no say in the choice of Emperor. Very often an emperor would choose his own successor, and some, like Vespasian and Trajan, were carried to power by the army. The Senate was only consulted, if at all, to confirm his election.

Under the Empire, government departments multiplied. It was civil servants, whom the emperor appointed and got rid of at will, who drew up rules which had all the force of law, and put them into operation. To be a senator was an honour which was increasingly granted to men of wealth and rank from the provinces, but they no longer had any real control. For though all the Roman officials – magistrates, consuls, tribunes, praetors, aediles and questors – were elected by the Senate, the candidates were drawn from a list put forward by the Emperor. The Senators themselves were not elected, but drawn from members of the Senatorial Order, which was made up of the wealthiest citizens. They shared among themselves high-sounding positions with little power. The Emperor allowed them to hold debates – but in the end, they had to do what he wanted. After Caesar, Rome was accustomed to accepting a master.

A session in the Senate during the Republic.

Citizens voting on a new law. Each one went through a wooden turnstile to cast their vote by putting a small wooden plaque in the urn. The plaque either bore the letter 'A' ('*Antiquo*' – 'I reject') or the letters UR ('*Uti rogas*' – 'I accept')

High-ranking citizens maintained 'clients', citizens who had no money, but had the right to vote. They looked after their patron's interests and acted as his electoral agents; in return they were given money and daily baskets of food.

Roman magistrates addressing the people in the Forum from the *Rostra*; a *rostrum* was the curved prow of a ship, and the *Rostra* was originally decorated with those, captured in the battle of Antium in 338 BC. Any citizen was supposed to have the right to speak here.

A convicted man hears the Emperor's verdict of death from a magistrate. Behind stand the *lictors*, carrying their *fasces*, an axe in a bundle of rods. Sometimes condemned men were offered the choice of execution or suicide.

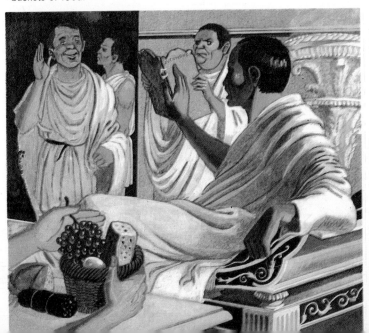

The Will of the Gods

The Romans believed in an after-life and in a whole host of gods and goddesses, called the Pantheon; they were thought to control and influence everything that happened to the Roman people, so it was very important to keep them happy, particularly Jupiter and Juno, the chief god and goddess, and Minerva, goddess of wisdom. To be on the safe side the Romans didn't hesitate to adopt foreign gods.

Roman worship consisted of a series of rites and ceremonies, conducted in and around the temples where the gods were supposed to live. Priests were responsible for the temple worship. This often consisted of making animal sacrifices, either to persuade the gods to give their help or to placate them if they were angry. These sacrifices were made at an altar outside the temple. The animals would be brought out, all prepared – fattened up, clean, glossy and decorated with garlands and ribbons. The worshippers wore laurel wreaths. After being paraded three times round the temple, the animals were killed. Then a priest called a *haruspex* 'took the auspices' by examining the entrails for supernatural signs. (The Romans had taken this practice from the Etruscans, an ancient people who lived in Italy before them.) Then the best parts of the animal were offered to the gods and the rest distributed to the worshippers.

As well as *haruspices* there were priests called augurs who interpreted the will of the gods by looking for signs in the sky, like lightning and the position of the stars, the flight of birds, and the way the sacred chickens ate their food. They also interpreted dreams.

All public events were accompanied by religious rites, and the Romans' beliefs entered into their daily life, too. People swore by Hercules and threatened by Jupiter. And if things weren't going too well, they understood that that was the will of the gods and that they must accept their destiny calmly, even if it meant death.

An animal sacrifice.

After a bull had been sacrificed and its blood sprinkled on the altar, its belly was slit open. The *haruspex* made a careful study of the entrails. People would consult him about the future and the liver, particularly, was thought to provide the answers.

The sacrificial bull was carefully cleaned, combed and curried. Assistants (*victimarii*) held it down so that its neck was offered to the priest making the sacrifice. The ritual axe was made of bronze, and the bull's blood was sprinkled on the altar.

Augurs were employed by the State to watch for signs expressing the will of the gods. Here an augur is watching some sacred chickens. If they eat greedily, letting food fall from their beaks, it's a good sign.

In the countryside, on wayside altars, people left other gifts for the gods when they wanted rain, or a good harvest. The gods were given the first bunch of ripe grapes, or the first sheaf of corn harvested.

Religious objects used for making sacrifices or offerings. They were made strictly according to tradition. The crook was carried by the augur and the knife was for cutting up sacrificial victims.

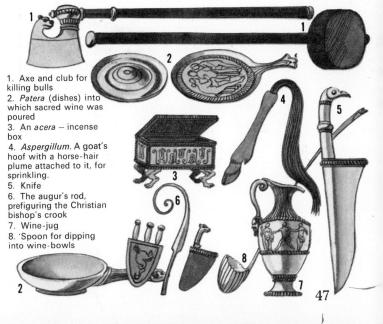

1. Axe and club for killing bulls
2. *Patera* (dishes) into which sacred wine was poured
3. An *acera* – incense box
4. *Aspergillum*. A goat's hoof with a horse-hair plume attached to it, for sprinkling.
5. Knife
6. The augur's rod, prefiguring the Christian bishop's crook
7. Wine-jug
8. Spoon for dipping into wine-bowls

47

On the Road

From the 2nd century BC onwards the Romans began building their great highways from Rome to all parts of the Empire. In England straight roads like the Fosse Way and Watling Street were originally built by Legionaries. Distances were calculated in miles – a Roman mile being a thousand (*millia*) military paces, or 1481·50 metres. The Golden Milestone stood in the Roman Forum. It was a marble column encased in bronze, inscribed in gold with the distances from Rome to other cities of the Empire.

Most roads in those times were narrow, made of rubble, and badly paved. Only the great State highways, the roads for which the Romans are famous, were arrow-straight and always in good repair. They were 4·15 metres wide, which allowed room for three chariots side by side.

Good roads were vital to the running of the Empire. Imperial messengers had to be able to travel fast with news and instructions, and if the peace was threatened the Legionaries had to be able to march to the trouble spot at top speed.

These highways were masterpieces of engineering. In Italy some of them included tunnels a kilometre long, lit by holes in the roof. A huge number of workmen were needed to build them.

The builders began by digging two parallel ditches on each side, to drain away excess water. Then they dug the foundations, down to rock or clay level, and put down a layer of sand and mortar. Four successive layers of stone and concrete were then laid down, totalling a depth of 1·5 metres. The surface was paved with flat stones and hard rocks. The road was slightly cambered, rising in the middle to let rain-water run down into the ditches each side. Roads like this were built to last – and last they did. At Wheeldale, near Whitby, we can still see the well preserved paving of the Roman road. It is traceable for 13 kilometres from Gawthorne Camps over the moor to Aislaby.

In London itself the only straight roads, Holborn – Oxford Street – Bayswater – Uxbridge, and Park Lane – Edgware, are both Roman.

Legionaries building a Roman highway.

The highways were ·used by Imperial officials and private citizens, travelling in fast two-horse wagons. One emperor was said to have fitted a revolving chair in his carriage so that he could get an all-round view of the scenery.

Silk was brought from China on camel-back over caravan routes across the Central Asian deserts. The Chinese sold it to the Parthians, who in turn sold it to the Romans. Silk was a luxury which was much sought after by the rich.

Inns offered rest and refreshment· all along the highways. Travellers could change their horses, get their vehicles repaired and buy provisions. These inns were built by the State, by local authorities and by private people.

The arrival of a general and his Legions gave townspeople a good excuse for some celebrations. The whole population would go to greet him and throw flowers to the soldiers as they marched along the road. After a procession, everyone would make for the temple, where a religious ceremony was held. Later, there would be a banquet, and the guests would drink toasts to the greatness of Rome and the health of the emperor.

Taking Food to Rome

There were 1,200,000 Romans to be fed daily, and the Italian countryside was cultivated less and less, so the State had a problem. All Rome's food supplies came from abroad by sea, and were unloaded at Ostia, the biggest port in the Empire. As the historian Tacitus wrote, 'Every day the life of the Roman people is at the mercy of the sea and storms.' The emperors Claudius and Trajan built the two harbours at Ostia, which covered an area of over a hundred hectares. They were protected by two stone jetties, and a lighthouse was built on an artificial island made by sinking a boat filled with rocks. The Romans built ports everywhere, where their commercial fleet could pick up supplies. Cities like Arles on the Rhône river in Gaul became huge storage depots where wool, timber and corn were brought from the north before being re-exported to Rome. Alexandria, in Egypt, was used in the same way.

Roman fleets sailed as far as the Black Sea, where they went to obtain timber and Scythian corn, and the North Sea, where there was a busy trade in wool and minerals. Ships were built of pine, oak or cedar, with nails of bronze. The hulls were caulked with tow and made watertight with pitch and wax, and painted over. The largest ships, like the heavy, round *Corbita*, were sailing vessels. Only light vessels were rowed by oarsmen.

Sea journeys were always long and difficult; the owners had a lot of money at stake, so they had their cargoes insured. When they reached their destination the merchants re-sold their wares to dealers and manufacturers. The produce was stored in huge warehouses, covering ten hectares at Ostia and many more in Rome. They were filled with candles, torches, parchment notebooks and rolls of papyrus, pepper and other spices, sheaves of corn, *amphorae* (earthenware jars) full of wine and oil, clothing, building materials – everything that was needed to maintain life in the biggest city of the western world.

Timber being unloaded at a Roman port.

Roman traders on the banks of the Nile buying up elephants' tusks from Africa. Ivory fetched high prices in Rome. Merchants also bought rhinoceros horns, which were ground to a powder for use in medicines.

Whenever possible goods were transported across Europe by river. It was more practical to use barrels than fragile *amphorae*. The barrels, made of oak and strengthened with iron hoops, were invented by the Gauls.

Egypt was one of the granaries of the ancient world. Here a scribe employed by a wealthy landowner is counting the sacks of grain the slaves are loading on to the ship for delivery to the great port of Alexandria.

From there they will be taken to Rome. Italy imported nearly all its provisions of corn and cereal.

Taking goods by road, in ox-drawn carts, could be a very slow business. Sometimes the loads weighed nearly 500 kilos, and accidents could happen! Here a cart full of empty jars has fallen off the edge of the road.

People preferred to go by sea or river on long journeys. The roads were used more frequently by the army and officials than for transporting goods.

The Growth of New Towns

All over the Empire, in towns and countryside alike, architects, surveyors and labourers were kept busy building and re-building roads, houses, public buildings and even whole towns and cities. The countries conquered by Rome had their own towns and capital cities, but the crudely built *oppida* (fortified towns) of Gaul and Britain could not compare with Rome in size or splendour. Wherever they settled the Romans built temples, baths, theatres and arenas. In Britain towns like Colchester and St Albans were completely re-planned with big stone buildings, imposing walls and gateways, and fine houses. All around the Mediterranean and northern Europe this urbanization led to great changes in people's way of life. The rich began to desert their huge country estates to live in these new towns where there was so much happening. As well as providing entertainment and social life, they were busy centres of trade.

From the reign of Augustus onwards whole towns were built in country districts to house retired Legionaries. Autun in France, Merida in Spain and Turin in Italy started in this way. The original population would consist of two or three thousand men and their families. New towns sprang up all over North Africa – like Timgad, founded by Trajan in Algeria, which was a model Roman city built on the grid pattern with finely paved streets and colonnades, and a triumphal arch in the centre.

Under the Pax Romana, society in all these urban centres was modelled on that of Rome. Men of wealth and rank sat on the local councils, making decisions about public spending, and giving employment to the local workers, many of whom came from country districts. Whether you were in Ephesus in Asia, Lyons in Gaul or Lepcis Magna in Libya, you knew that you were in a Roman city. And in the evenings the plebeian crowd in the Forum could have been taken for the plebeians of Rome – unemployed, talkative and eager for distractions.

A surveyor plotting the line of an aqueduct.

A Legionary guarding the gates of Trier in Germany. Service in the North was hard and some soldiers bribed their centurions to evade their duties. Centurions were not popular; they could hit out with their vinestaffs at the slightest breach of discipline.

Theatres were built in all the large cities of the Empire. Putting on a play demanded a lot of preparation. In hot countries sailors put up huge awnings to protect the audience from the sun, like that over the Colosseum in Rome.

A winter scene on the Rhine frontier. The Legionaries built garrison towns, with wooden houses called *cannabae*. The soldiers were recruited from the Gauls, the Britons (who were considered very warlike), and even from

The Roman garrisons stationed in Africa used to hunt lions in the hinterland. Sometimes lions would come down from the Atlas mountains and attack the cattle belonging to farms. The soldiers organized proper hunts, using lances to kill the lions.

German tribes. Only the officers spoke Latin. Garrison towns attracted trade, and the surrounding countryside was cultivated to feed the troops. What started as a temporary camp became the nucleus of a new town.

Togas, Tunics and Sandals

The Romans did not have the kind of under-clothes we are familiar with – pants, vests and socks. The only undergarment worn by both sexes was a tunic, knee-length for men, ankle-length for girls and women. In the early days of the Republic men just wore a loin-cloth under their toga.

The toga, which seems to have been Etruscan in origin, was the only garment worn by the ancient Romans and was a mark of citizenship. Those worn by magistrates and boys had a purple band round the edge. This garment, called the *toga praetexta*, was worn by boys up to the age of sixteen, when they took on the plain white toga of manhood. During the Empire people began to find the toga inconvenient, and gave it up except for special ceremonial occasions, or at the Senate. In its place they wore the *pallium*, a light-weight cloak draped over the tunic. The tunic itself became the outer garment, and was put on over an undertunic, often called a *camisia* (from which the words 'chemise' and 'camisole' come). The tunic might have sewn sleeves attached to it. As a result of foreign influences, particularly from Gaul, some people began to adopt narrow breeches, a heavy cloak called a *paenula*, made of thick natural wool or leather, and the *caracalla*, a cloak with a hood attached.

Women also wore a long tunic, the *stola*, over an under-tunic tied in at the waist. When they went out they also put on a draped mantle, like a shawl, the *palla*. Unlike the men, women could wear clothes dyed in bright colours.

Romans hardly ever wore hats, but women carried fans, and sometimes sunshades.

How to put a toga on

Starting off as a simple wrap, the toga got bigger and bigger until it had a 6 metre diameter. Of course, it was impossible to put it on by yourself, and you had to have someone to help you!

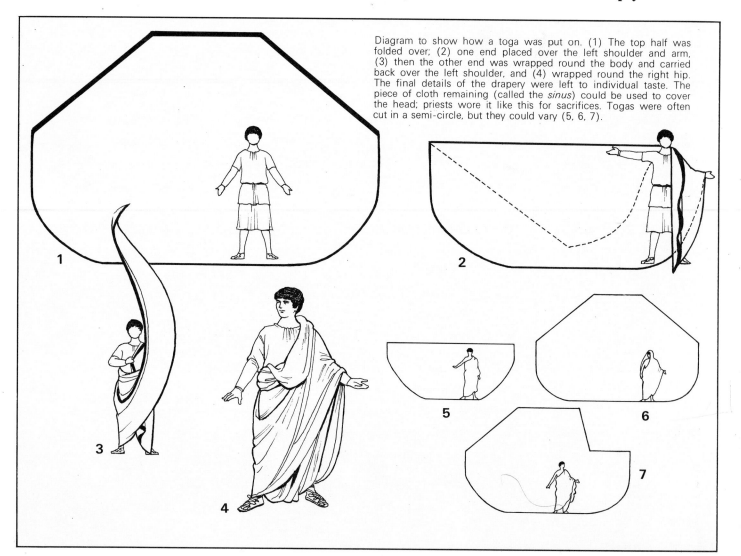

Diagram to show how a toga was put on. (1) The top half was folded over; (2) one end placed over the left shoulder and arm, (3) then the other end was wrapped round the body and carried back over the left shoulder, and (4) wrapped round the right hip. The final details of the drapery were left to individual taste. The piece of cloth remaining (called the *sinus*) could be used to cover the head; priests wore it like this for sacrifices. Togas were often cut in a semi-circle, but they could vary (5, 6, 7).

A

B

C

D

Women's hairstyles varied from period to period, and were often very elaborate. Sometimes the hair wasn't thick enough for the current style and then wigs would be worn. (A) This complicated structure of plaits piled on top of the head was worn by young girls on their wedding day. (B) and (C) The 'bird's-nest' or 'diadem' style appeared under the Flavians, and lasted a long time, with variations. (D) An early hairstyle. Until the middle of the first century, styles remained fairly simple.

E1

E2

E3

F

(E1) A long-sleeved tunic was put on first, and over it (E2) a shorter tunic with short sleeves. (E3) The outfit was completed by a cloak fastened with a buckle on the right shoulder.

(F) Women's tunics often had sleeves fastened with buckles. The over garment was often sleeveless, and a cloak would be worn over it. All these garments were dyed in different colours, usually quite bright ones.

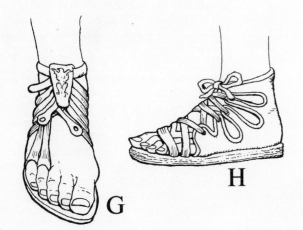
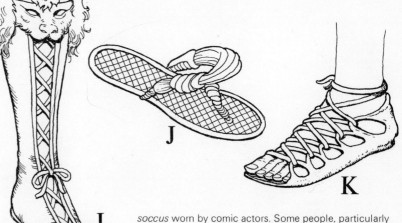

G

H

I

J

K

(G, H) The most common form of footwear was the sandal, laced across the instep. (I) Boots like this, called a *cothurnus* or huskin, were regarded as divine garments and were supposed to be worn by the gods. Some emperors wore them too. In the theatre they were associated with tragedy, in contrast to the flat *soccus* worn by comic actors. Some people, particularly soldiers and wagoners, wore short ankle-length boots *(peronis)*. (J) Philosophers and people who believed in the simple life wore light sandals, often made of papyrus. (K) the *cartabina*, also laced across the top, was worn by peasants.

Animals
Wild and Tame

BEWARE OF THE DOG

In the year 79 the volcano Vesuvius erupted, destroying the Roman cities of Herculaneum and Pompeii, and killing thousands of people including the famous historian Pliny. Hundreds of years later these cities were dug up by archaeologists. And it was in Pompeii that they came across an inscription saying '*Cave Canem*' – 'Beware of the Dog'. It was just the sort of notice people still put up today to warn visitors that the house is guarded by a fierce dog. Dogs were used for other purposes too, in the

Roman Empire. There were huge mastiffs who kept watch over public buildings day and night. There were vast numbers of strays who helped to clean the streets of rubbish by eating up waste scraps of food. Some dogs, usually greyhounds, were kept as pets and could be seen going for walks with their rich patrician owners. And it is possible that there were guide-dogs for the blind; what looks like a painting of one was discovered in the excavation of Herculaneum. In Sicily about a thousand dogs were kept around the temple of the god Adranus; when guests at the lavish feasts had had too much wine to drink, these dogs were trained to guide them back to their homes. Dogs were also used, as today, for hunting game. But the most unusual – and the most unkind – use which the Romans thought up for dogs was to make them carry secret messages, between fellow accomplices in a conspiracy, for instance. The unfortunate beast was made to swallow a metal tube, in which the message was enclosed. This was also its death sentence, for when the animal arrived at its destination the only way to recover the precious tube was to kill it. It does seem that the Romans were grateful to these unlucky and over-faithful servants, for dog cemeteries have been found in which the skeletons have coins lying beside them, doubtless placed there in gratitude for 'services rendered'.

Many of the most highly valued hounds came from Britain.

PIGEONS

There is nothing new about pigeon-fancying and carrier pigeons. Before the Romans, the Assyrians and the Medes used pigeons to carry messages during their military campaigns, and the Greeks used them to broadcast the names of the Olympic Games winners to all the city-states within Greece.

The Romans, too, bred large numbers of these winged messengers in huge pigeon-cotes built on the roofs of their houses. And they were not only used to carry messages – pigeons were also considered to be very good to eat, although the true gourmets of the Empire preferred doves.

In several parts of the Empire, pigeon relays were kept in constant

readiness, in order to spread important news, particularly after the creation of the first 'air mail' during the reign of the Emperor Diocletian in the third century AD. But well before that time, pigeons were of military value; in 43 BC, when Brutus was besieged in Modena by Mark Antony, he used carrier-pigeons to communicate with his allies.

DOLPHINS

Many of the Roman coins that have been found have the picture of a dolphin engraved on them. The Mediterranean sea was full of dolphins in those days, and from the earliest times they attracted the attention of human beings by their friendly behaviour towards sailors. Meeting a school of dolphins on a voyage was regarded as a good omen. Only the people of Thrace hunted them, and for that the Greeks and Romans strongly disapproved of them.

It is easy to understand, then, why these mammals were closely linked with all the legends about the sea-gods.

When Neptune was wooing Amphitrite, for instance, he sent a dolphin to fetch her, and rewarded it for its services by placing in the sky the constellation of ten stars called the Dolphin. And there were also many

tales, some no doubt exaggerated, about dolphins rescuing sailors or letting children ride on their backs. Stories like this are told in Pliny's *Natural History*. The earliest Romans, like the Greeks, knew a great deal about the habits and behaviour of dolphins. It was said that you only needed to call 'Simon, Simon!' and the dolphin would respond – even though the call was nothing like its own ultra-sonic language. The name 'Simon' in fact comes from a Greek word meaning 'snub-nose', and dolphins were traditionally called by this nickname.

DIVINATION AND SUPERSTITION

Many of the elaborate religious rites practised by the Romans came originally from the Etruscans, particularly the custom of trying to

understand the wishes of the gods by interpreting natural phenomena. Methods included examining the entrails of sacrificed animals for special signs, in particular the liver, whose colour and shape varies very much from one animal to another. And they

also foretold the future by 'taking the auspices', which consisted of observing the behaviour of birds. For example, they took note of the way in which crows or vultures flew, and how the sacred chickens pecked at their food. During the First Punic War the commander of the Roman fleet, Claudius Pulcher, took some chickens on board with him so that he could 'question' them on the voyage as to the best course of action to follow. The chickens were probably upset by the sea crossing; anyway, they refused to eat the grain they were offered – a bad sign. In a fury, Claudius Pulcher threw them overboard, crying 'Let them drink, then, if they won't eat!' When his fleet was beaten by the Carthaginians, the Romans blamed his irreligious behaviour for the defeat.

Extracts from the Letters of Cassius Octavius of Arretium (59–125 AD)

'First letter from Cassius to his friend Lucius'

Concerning Oracles

I am writing to you from Rome, where I came to see the games the Emperor Domitian has been giving in the Colosseum. I saw a rhinoceros fighting there – the emperor was so delighted with it that he has had special medals struck with pictures of a rhinoceros on them! I don't intend to stay here long, for there are many disturbing rumours going round just now. The augurs have told the emperor that disasters are about to happen, and there are whispers of a conspiracy in his circle.

I must tell you, however, that I don't really believe in these predictions. Like Lucretius, I believe that man should be made to give up such superstitions. Is it really right for the State to let its decisions depend on the appetite of some sacred chickens? Cicero has already expressed his doubts about such methods.

At the festival of Lupercalia I watched the priests sacrificing dogs and goats, and cutting their hides into strips. Then, covered in goatskins, they ran after the women who'd come there hoping to be cured of sterility, striking them with these strips of hide. I don't know whether you've ever had occasion to attend the animal sacrifices which are supposed to attract the favour of the gods. The Greeks, Cretans, and Hebrews too, they say, decorate their bulls and cows with flowers and then cut their throats; sometimes they even sprinkle themselves with the blood. I would much rather watch the sport in which horse-men catch the bulls by the horns and throw them to the ground. That's a custom that has come to us from Crete, too, apparently, but I find it more dignified than those blood-baths our priests indulge in on their stone altars. I realise that you may be offended by my scepticism. But do you really believe that the 'Sacred Spring' which the Senate decreed at the start of the Second Punic War had any influence on the fate of our armies? Putting to death all the animals born during the spring didn't stop Hannibal from crushing our forces at the battles of Trebia, Trasimene and Cannae. Of course, it's true that in the end our general Scipio won the war for us at Zama. . . .

'First letter from Cassius to his sister Julia'

Remedies for Insect Bites

I have been extremely worried ever since I got your letter telling me that you were bitten by a spider hidden among vegetables from the garden. Do you know what kind of spider it was? In Apulia, particularly in the region of Tarentum, there are a lot of dangerous spiders called tarantulas. Or could it be one of those *phalangia*[1] Pliny writes about? – This seems more likely, since they are to be found among vegetables. The best remedy for the fever and dizziness which result from their bites is – as you probably know – to crush the body of the spider on the wound, or if that's impossible, cover the place with a piece of its web. Although you tell me you are now better, I am still concerned about you, for Pliny says that a spider bite can also make a woman barren. So I advise you to come to Rome as soon as you can, and we will go together to make a sacrifice at the temple of the Great Mother[2], the Eastern goddess who is famous for bestowing fertility.

I have been looking through my books to try to find something which might offer you some relief from your ills, and have come across several remedies you ought to know about. I have re-read the treatise by Discorides Petanius 'On Medical Matters'; he recommends castor, the musk secreted from the glands of beavers, as a remedy for ulcers, and to counteract the effects of snakes' venom and poisons from other animals and plants. That's a useful remedy, my dear sister, and so are those Pliny gives, using frogs as an ingredient, which I give you as well: A broth made of shrimps, flour and frogs boiled in wine is excellent for anyone who has lost weight and is suffering from physical fatigue. Crushed frogs, steeped in wine, are also very good against the poison of salamanders and toads. Finally, to cure the kind of fever which comes round every four days, known as the quartan fever, Pliny recommends us to eat the flesh of frogs cooked in olive oil.

Give my greetings to your husband Marcus, and my good wishes to yourself.

1. The malmignatte, a species of spider found in Provence, Italy and Corsica.
2. Cybele, originally an Asian goddess.

Animals for Circus Games

I write to you from Thamagus[1] in Africa, where I have been sent by the Emperor Trajan to organize the capture of wild beasts. For our unemployed, who have to be kept amused to avoid trouble, are costing us a great deal in animals of all kinds. The public is demanding ever more outlandish forms of entertainment. They have grown weary of panthers harnessed in chariots, or elephants kneeling down to write the emperor's name with their trunks in the sand of the Circus Maximus. They have had enough of gladiators fighting with lions. What they want today is armies of bears fighting buffalos, or bulls doing battle with rhinoceroses. Marcus, whom you know, tells me that he witnessed a revolting scene at the Colosseum: the head of a gladiatorial training school flogged a naked man to force him to separate a huge bear from a wild German bull which it was chained to. Three men died before a fourth succeeded, only to be trampled and torn to death in his turn. Marcus also tells me that at Lugdunum he saw women tied to the horns of bulls which were maddened by archers shooting arrows at them. The *mansuetarii*[2] of the Circus Maximus told me that they had found a way of enraging the elephants they put in to fight with bulls and rhinoceroses; they make them drink a concoction of rice and reeds before the fight. In the Colosseum they prefer to stick flaming brands in their flanks – the public enjoys that method more. I find

these games very cruel, but they say that they serve to maintain peace inside the Empire. But for how much longer, my dear Donatius?

It is all the more worrying because at the rate things are going, wild animals are proving more and more difficult to catch. In several regions some of them have completely disappeared – like the hippopotamus in Nubia and the elephant in North Africa, from where I am writing to you.

I have therefore had to search far and wide through our province of Mauretania[3] and organize several hunts to fulfil the emperor's wishes. We shall be sending him several hundred cheetahs, panthers and lions, and two hundred buffalos; also some ostriches and antelopes for his gardens. He already has over eleven thousand beasts in his menageries, and his *custodes vivarii*[4] are not short of work.

Our local Roman colonists have given me a great deal of assistance in the capture of these animals. They lent me their nets, for I had not brought enough with me to surround the hunting grounds – which is the method we use when we want to capture a large number of animals at a time. When the nets have been put in place, huntsmen on horseback drive the beasts towards these enclosures, using lances, stones and long sticks with a tuft of bright red feathers at the top. The animals are completely terrified. They are caught by beaters, protected with shields and brandishing flaming

torches, who shut them into huge open-work crates. Over twenty of my men have been killed or injured since I have been here, and we have had to destroy a good hundred beasts that were too ferocious to take. I have asked the emperor to send me reinforcements, since I am now obliged to go down south to capture elephants, rhinoceroses and hippopotami, and possibly giraffes as well – the emperor being very fond of these. But I must confess that I take no pleasure in all this carnage, and I am longing to get back to my villa at Arretium, and my peacocks. On the journey home I shall probably make a detour by Corsica to see what has become of the pheasants from Trapezus[5] which we let loose there to see if they would acclimatize.

My good wishes to you.

1. Timgad.
2. Elephant trainers. They taught the elephants tricks such as kneeling down, fighting like gladiators, dancing to the sound of cymbals, and so on.
3. Modern Morocco and western Algeria.
4. Keepers of the Imperial menageries.
5. Trebizond, on the Black Sea coast in the Roman province of Cappadocia.

Invaded by Rabbits

I see from your letter that your stay in Gallia Narbonensis[1] has enabled you to see for yourself the amount of damage done to the crops by rabbits, and that you still haven't found any way to destroy them. However, you know how much importance the emperor places on keeping our colonists in those parts happy. I believe that the best way to begin would be to clear the *leporaria*, the rabbit warrens referred to by Gellius and Varro[2]; this will prevent these vermin from breeding.

Apparently the situation in the Balearic Isles is even more disastrous. My father tells me that one day the local settlers sent a delegation to the emperor Augustus, asking his permission to leave the islands for somewhere more secure, for the plague of rabbits was threatening to reduce them to famine. But all the emperor did was to send them some ferrets so that they could get rid of the pests themselves. At the same time he sent several hundred ferrets to the province of Tarraconensis[3], which Catullus[4] described as *cuniculosa*[5], so riddled was it with burrows. They were quite ineffective, and when I went out there last year I could see that even the roots of trees had been gnawed away. I do sympathise with you, my dear Lucius, for having let yourself in for this imperial mission. Whatever you do, make sure your house is well protected, for Pliny tells us that it was rabbits that brought down the ramparts of Tarragona, by digging more and more burrows underneath them. Pray to the goddess Diana to spare you a similar misfortune . . . and to aid you in your task.

1. Roman province in the south of Gaul.
2. Gellius was a historian of the 1st century BC. Varro, who lived at the same time, was the author of a treatise on agriculture, *Res rusticae* (*Country Matters*).
3. A Roman province including the greater part of Spain.
4. A Latin poet of the 1st century BC.
5. Overrun with rabbits.

On Animal Husbandry

I have returned for a few months to my villa at Arretium, and have no shortage of work, for people come from far and wide to ask my advice on the best methods of looking after animals.

I shall never understand why so many people want to breed peacocks for the dinner table. I myself find peacock flesh very unpleasant, and would much prefer to look at them spreading their tails in my gardens. Nor do I understand people's dislike of quails; they breed them but don't eat them because they mistakenly believe them to be poisonous. I am having a few sent to you; serve them to Marcus garnished with Smyrna grapes. I am also sending you some edible dormice (my *gliraria*[1] are full of them) which are delicious roasted in honey.

Servus, who looks after my *piscinae*[2], says that the eels should be fished more often, for they are not as fat as formerly. Thanks to the gods, all my herds are healthy. I am expecting several hundred geese, which Rufus is sending me from Gallia Narbonensis; he is also sending some to Rome. Since they are arriving on foot, however, I doubt whether I can let you have any fattened goose-livers for a while.

I am going to make use of the time I have to spend here by building a *cochlearium*[3] on the little island in the middle of the river. I have been told that that is the best place to have it, to prevent the snails from escaping. Snail-breeding is not at all expensive. All you have to do is to ensure a supply of water by building a small aqueduct and a ramp; the water has to fall on to a large, flat stone so that it splashes all the surrounding area and maintains the level of humidity the snails need. As for their food, other snail-breeders tell me that all they need is a little bran and a supply of laurel leaves.

I am sorry that I am far from the sea, for I cannot keep *muraenae*[4] alive in the fresh water of my ponds. I would also like to be able to breed oysters. The ones that come to us from Aquitania[5] are very expensive. I have re-read what Pliny has to say about the oyster beds that Sergius Orata laid down in Capania near Baia on Lake Lucrine. To feed them he had shellfish brought from the coast round Brindisi and even from Gaul. On the Adriatic coast, near Aquileia[6], I was able to see how the fishermen set about catching fine oysters. They throw bundles of wood into the waters of the natural oyster-beds. Three years later they pull them out, and the faggots are covered with huge shells filled with succulent flesh.

I forgot to tell you that during my absence Servus acquired a donkey. But I want to get rid of it, for I suspect Servus of being a disciple of the man called Christ – they say that his followers worship donkeys. I have also brought back from Rome a big Alexandrian parrot for my wife Claudia. I dare not tell you how much I paid for it – it cost me the price of a slave!

1. Dormouse enclosures.
2. Fish-ponds.
3. Snail-pens.
4. A sea fish the Romans were very fond of.
5. Province in southern Gaul.
6. A big Roman town near Trieste, which was destroyed by Attila the Hun. Its inhabitants founded Venice.

Concerning Bears

You ask me to bring you back a pair of bears or panthers. So you, too, have succumbed to the popular craze for keeping wild animals! May I remind you that an ancient decree of our aediles, going back five hundred years, forbids anyone to keep dogs, pigs, boars, bears, panthers and lions in any place where people live, unless they are kept on a strong chain. It is true that these days no-one takes any notice of it. In view of our friendship I will fulfil your request in regard to the panthers, but I really must advise you against keeping bears. They are cunning creatures, and I have done a lot of reading about them.

Did you know that Scipio Africanus, to celebrate his victory over Hannibal at Zama, offered the Romans the spectacle of a battle between forty bears and sixty-three panthers? Those were brown bears, but it is said that when Ptolemy V, King of Egypt, was crowned at around the same time, the crowd witnessed the sight of a huge white bear[1] among the animals in the procession. For my own part, I have never captured a bear of this kind, but I have hunted brown bears in our provinces of Germany, Tarraconensis

and Mauretania Caesariensis.[2] In Mauretania they were trapped in pits and cloths were thrown over their heads to make them less fierce. In Germany I have seen them trapped in birdlime, but this had to be an extremely strong mix and the hunters were not willing to give me the secret of its composition.

Our emperors have always liked to own lions and tigers, doubtless because, like their subjects, they can stand up on their hind legs. Augustus's menageries contained only a dozen, but they say that Caligula had over five hundred in his. Nero, one day, sent a troop of his horseguard into the Colosseum to fight with four hundred bears. He also liked to have bears fight with seals, which was not a pretty sight. They covered the poor creatures with a thick, sticky coat of birdlime. When they rolled about on the ground trying to get it off their bodies became covered with the flowers, leaves and straw which the crowd threw down into the arena. Sometimes Nero let the bears loose on those followers of Christ who refused to renounce their beliefs, but in the end he gave this up, for once their victims had fallen to the

ground the bears took no further notice of them.

You also say in your letter that Flavius has made you the gift of a lion which comes and eats out of your hand. I recommend you to have it shorn, as the emperor has done with his. Leave only the mane and narrow strips of hair down the back of the legs and along the flanks. And tell the person who does the shearing to leave a big tuft between the shoulders. If you should ever go to Capua, go and see the lions owned by Ennius, that pedant who doesn't know what to do with his money. He has had their manes sprinkled with gold dust, and puts them into jewelled harnesses to draw him round the countryside in his chariot. He doubtless wishes to imitate Mark Antony, who appeared in Rome in a similar equipage after his journey from Brindisi.

My good wishes to you.

1. Probably an albino brown bear and not a polar bear.
2. Morocco and Algeria.

How to Shoe Horses and Mules

You ask me about the origin of the *solea* which the Emperor Nero and his favourite Poppaea put on the feet of their mules. I haven't seen them myself; Suetonius says that Nero's mules were shod with silver soles, and according to Pliny, Poppaea's with gold. What I do know is that these sorts of sandal are only attached to horses' hoofs when the roads are rough, for our compatriots who appreciate horses for the hardness and thickness of their hoofs like to hear the sound of chargers clanging like cymbals on paved roads. On this subject, Columella[1] recommends that stable floors should be paved with oak,

because this kind of wood hardens the horses' hoofs as stones do. He also recommends that their feet should be fitted with shoes of plaited broom, but I don't know the reason for this . . . I know of your passion for horsemanship, my dear nephew, and while I am writing to you I would like to give you some advice, in case you should be thinking of taking it up as a career. Our post-horse service is so well organized that there are scarcely any openings for you there. As for the army cavalry, it has a very poor reputation, for it has never shone in battle. Although it is not nearly large enough, with scarcely 100 *equites*[2] to a legion,

the emperor does nothing to strengthen it. He prefers to place his trust in mercenaries from Numidia, Gaul and Germany. We are far from the days of Caligula, who had such a passion for horses that he made his own horse Incitatus a consul . . . I would therefore advise you rather to take up breeding. Read Virgil again; he speaks of it in his *Georgics*; and, if such is your wish, I can write to my friend Demotius and ask him to employ you next year in the stud farm at Hadrumetum[3] in Africa.

1. A writer on animal husbandry in the 1st century.
2. Horsemen.
3. Now Sousse in Tunisia.

On the Art of Pleasing One's Guests by Serving Them Choice Dishes

You ask my advice about the banquet you wish to give for your friends.

Although Cicero claimed that 'the least respectable of all professions are those of fishmonger, butcher, cook and sauce-maker', in my opinion one of the greatest pleasures is to please one's guests by serving them nothing but the choicest of dishes. You may be familiar with the poet Juvenal's description of what should appear at a banquet worthy of the name – 'a huge lobster garnished with asparagus, a mullet from Corsica, the finest lamprey that the Straits of Sicily can provide, a goose liver, a capon as big as a house, a piping hot boar, truffles and apples.' But I myself prefer the more delicate menus suggested by Apicius in his cookery book. (You can find it in the two public libraries founded by the Emperor Augustus.) Which of your friends, for example, would not be extremely pleased to see on the menu, that they were going to be served with the following feast:

The gustatio
Salt fish and eggs
Stuffed sow's udders
Medaillon of calves' brains
cooked in milk and eggs
Boiled mushrooms with a hot
fish-stock sauce
Sea urchins cooked with spices,
honey and a sauce of oil and eggs

The cena
Roast venison with onion sauce
Jericho dates, grapes, oil and honey
Ostrich, boiled, with a sweet sauce
Dove boiled in its feathers
Roast parrot
Dormice stuffed with pork and
pigeons
Boiled ham with figs and
laurel leaves, dipped in honey
and cooked in a pastry crust
Flamingo boiled with dates

For the secunda mensa
Fricassee of roses with pastries
Pitted dates stuffed with nuts and
pine-kernels and fried in honey
Hot African cakes with sweet wine,
served with honey

Some key dates in Roman History

BC

753	Commonly accepted date for Foundation of Rome. Romans generally dated events as being in such a year 'AUC', '*Ab Urbe Condita*', 'From the Foundation of the City', or sometimes by the name of a Consul of the year in question.
753–509	Rome ruled by kings, first four Romans, then three Etruscans. The Etruscans were a powerful, cultivated people, who dominated the territory immediately north of the Tiber. Their origin is uncertain. They humbled Rome more than once, but by the second century they were reduced to assimilation with their Roman victors.
509	Rome is a republic, whose chief magistrates are two consuls, appointed annually. During the next two and a half centuries Rome gradually expands her hegemony over the whole of Italy, the conquest of the whole peninsula being completed in 266. Numerous 'colonies' planted, that is, purely Roman enclaves in non-Roman environments. The system was later introduced throughout the empire.
390	Romans defeated by Gauls at the Allia. Rome, except the Capitol, captured and burnt. Gauls bribed to depart.
280–275	War with Pyrrhus of Epirus and with South Italy. Rome finally wins.
264–241	The first of the three PUNIC WARS against Carthage.
218–201	Second Punic War, with Hannibal in Italy; but Rome again after terrible reverses wins in the end.
214–168	Three Macedonian wars, which ultimately give Greece to Rome.
149–146	Third Punic War. Rome destroys Carthage.
107	Marius popular general throws open the army to all citizens.
81–44	Decline and eclipse of Republic through civil strife.

58–51	Julius Caesar conquers Gaul, and twice raids Britain.
44	Assassination of Julius Caesar.
31	Battle of Actium makes Octavius, later Augustus, First Roman Emperor.

AD

43	Claudius sends Aulus Plautius with four legions to subdue Britain. Caractacus, king of the Silures, overpowered. Colchester taken.
44	'Britannia' becomes Roman province. Mendip lead mines already in Roman hands. Legionary fortresses at Gloucester and Lincoln. Invasion of South Wales.
51	Caractacus finally defeated in North Wales, flees to Cartimandua, queen of the Brigantes, and is surrendered to Romans.
61	Icenian revolt under Boudicca (Boadicea) suppressed, after sack of Colchester, London and St Alban's.
71–74	Brigantes conquered. Legionary fortress at York.
78–84	Agricola subdues Britain as far north as Forth-Clyde. Caledonians defeated at Mons Graupius. Roman fleet circumnavigates Britain. Legionary fortress at Inchtuthill, beyond the Tay. Most northerly post ever established by Roman arms. Evacuated c. 90.
85	Domitian recalls Agricola.
122	Hadrian visits Britain. Construction of 'Hadrian's Wall' from Tyne to Solway begun.
139–142	Q. Lollius Urbicus, governor under Antoninus Pius, advances into Scotland and builds Antonine Wall across Clyde-Forth isthmus.
211	Emperor Septimius Severus, campaigning against revolting Britons, dies at York. His sons Caracalla and Gaeta proclaimed there as his joint successors.
306	Constantine hailed as emperor at York.
407	Roman troops withdrawn from Britain.

Overseas, or 'imperial', expansion began with the First Punic War★ in 240 BC. The remaining provinces were added as follows:

BC

231	**Sardinia and Corsica**
197	**Spain (two provinces, later three)** *after Second Punic War★*
146	**Macedonia and Achaia (i.e. Greece) Northern Africa Carthaginian possessions** *after Third Punic War★*
133–129	**Asia, i.e. Asia Minor**
121–118	**Southern Gaul** *known as the Province par excellence: still called 'Provence' to-day. Dalmatia added by Augustus★*
81	**Gaul south of Alps**
74	**Bithynia**
67	**Cyrene and Crete**
66	**Cilicia**
64	**Syria**
63	**Pontus** *added to Bithynia after death of king Mithradates*
63	**Judaea**
58	**Cyprus**

58–51	**Gaul beyond Alps** *three provinces, besides Southern Gaul after AD 17 united with Northern Africa treated as private domain of emperor*
46	**Numidia**
30	**Egypt**
29	**Moesia (Lower Danube)**
25	**Galatia & Pamphylia** *Paphlagonia soon added*
15	**Rhaetia & Noricum (Upper Danube)**

AD

10	**Pannonia (Middle Danube)**
17	**Cappadocia**
40	**Mauretania**
44	**Britain south of Thames**
44–54	**Lycia and Rhodes**
106–116	**Dacia, Armenia, Eastern Arabia, Mesopotamia** *Won by Trajan but, except Dacia, given up by successor Hadrian. N.B. The Roman Empire reached its greatest extent under Trajan.*

★ See Above

Index